Handprint
and make your own
Bags

Handprint
and make your own
Bags

35 stylish projects using stencils, lino cuts, and more

Jenny McCabe

CICO BOOKS

LONDON NEW YORK

To my ever supportive
husband Ben, my beautiful,
brilliant children Jesse and
Joe, and my wonderful
friend Ron.

Published in 2013 by CICO Books
An imprint of Ryland Peters & Small Ltd
519 Broadway, 5th Floor,
New York NY 10012
20–21 Jockey's Fields,
London WC1R 4BW

www.cicobooks.com

10 9 8 7 6 5 4 3 2 1

A CIP catalog record for this book is
available from the Library of Congress
and the British Library.

ISBN: 978-1-908862-64-8

Printed in China

Editor: Lindsay Kaubi
Designer: Lucy Parissi
Photographer: Claire Richardson
Stylists: Tanya Goodwin and Carol Wortley
Illustrators: Step-by-step illustrations by
Carrie Hill and templates by Simon Roulstone

For digital editions, visit
www.cicobooks.com/apps.php

contents

introduction

I have always made things; I can't bring myself to buy a new bag when I know I can make one. When I was a little girl doing my chores, ironing was a joy to me because I learnt so much about garment construction just from seeing how the seams worked and the shape of the pattern pieces. My top tip would be to "stay curious," I continue to be fascinated with fabric and how it works, I have been known to take apart a favorite old bag or dress just to see how it was put together.

In this book I hope to share with you some of the tips and tricks I've picked up along the way and set you off on your own journey, printing your own fabric and making your own bags.

All the prints in this book are designed to demonstrate the basic hand-printing techniques and inspire you to have a go. There is very little specialty or expensive equipment needed, and everything should be available from your local art store.

Everything in this book is transferable, the print designs can go on any bag, the same bag shape can look very different with another print or in a different color scheme. Mix and match to make the project that's perfect for you.

There are easy projects in this book and some real challenges; I hope that you will feel confident to move up through the levels learning new skills as you go.

PRACTICAL ADVICE

When choosing fabrics for the projects in this book, look for things like strong cottons and linens, denims or canvas. For most bags you will need a strong fabric; even for the more delicate bags, you still need a fabric that will hold its shape and not rip if you put your keys inside.

design and inspiration

Inspiration for your own print designs will come from all around you, keep your eyes and mind open. Check out the high-street stores, fashion and interior magazines, and look in thrift stores for vintage fabrics, wallpapers, ceramics, books, and magazines. All of these things may inspire you. A walk in a park to collect leaves, flowers and objects, photos of shadows and shapes, architecture—look at the big scene and the tiny detail, there is pattern and shape everywhere, you just need to look for it.

MOOD BOARDS

A mood board is a great way to keep all of your inspiration in one place, so that you can see what ideas develop. A mood board can be a physical board with images pinned to it or a digital file with all of your images collected together.

SKETCHBOOKS

If you keep a sketchbook and spend a lot of time playing and drawing in it, the ideas will flow. Draw with different media—pencils, paintbrushes, sticks dipped in ink; the experimentation will help you to find new shapes and marks that will end up as your print designs.

PATTERN TYPES

When you are coming up with your designs, consider whether your print is going to be a repeated pattern or a single motif. Are you going to build up a pattern randomly or have a regular, square repeat? Consider the scale of the design and how it will be spaced out on the fabric. All of these decisions will influence your final designs.

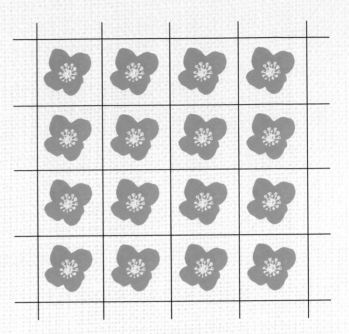

Square repeat

Half-drop repeat

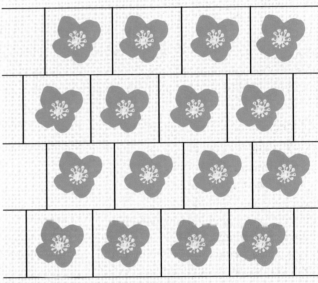

Brick repeat

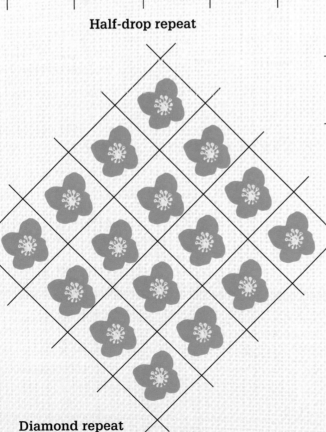

Diamond repeat

Scales repeat

printing techniques

The projects in this book are designed to introduce you to the different printing techniques. Once you feel confident, you can design your own prints and you can, of course, change any of the projects in this book. Just pick a bag shape and a print design and away you go.

You can put your print design onto blocks, plates, rollers, stamps, or stencils. When deciding what to use, consider the size of the design and whether you are likely to need to make other things with the print. Stencils will only last a short time and then need to be re-made, rubber stamps, if cared for, will last for hundreds of prints. Each technique has its pros and cons, and you will also have your own favorite that you choose to use the most.

Don't be afraid to have a go, and remember that mistakes and imperfections add to the beauty and unique nature of handprinted items.

Basic printing equipment

- Newspaper
- Water
- Clothes
- Sponges—you'll need plenty
- Sponge rollers/brayers
- Old jars or plastic pots for mixing and storing paint
- Apron
- Sharp scissors
- Sharp knife
- Cutting board
- Masking tape
- Hair dryer
- A good printing surface—flat with no lumps

The printing techniques

Block printing

A surface where areas are carved away to make the design, coated with paint, and applied to the fabric with pressure.

Potato printing—A technique we all remember from childhood, but not to be dismissed because you can achieve some amazing results. You can work with potatoes, or sweet potatoes, or apples, or any veg that will provide a smooth, flat surface and is easy to carve. Once you have carved your design into the vegetable, load paint onto the surface with a sponge or a soft brush and print, applying even pressure to the back of the vegetable. Take care not to load too much paint on your block or you will have rough and messy edges to your print. This method is only good for short printing runs, because the vegetable will dry up and rot.
Tools—Vegetables, sharp knife, sponge.

Potato printing

Lino printing

Erasers and rubber block

Lino printing—This is a classic technique; the design is drawn onto the lino sheet and the areas that you do not want to be printed are carved away with sharp lino cutting tools. The paint is loaded onto the lino with a sponge roller and printed onto the fabric by applying even pressure to the back with either a clean roller or you hands. Lino printing is great for building up layers and, if cared for, the lino sheet will last a long time, so you can use it for many projects. Take care when carving because lino tools are very sharp and you do have to apply a lot of pressure to get through the lino. Always carve away from your body and hands.

Tools—Lino sheet, lino cutters, sharp knife, sponge roller, clean roller/brayer.

Erasers and rubber block—This is a funky way to create prints; you can use any flat erasers from the stationery store, or buy sheets of rubber that you can carve your design into to make larger prints. It is similar to lino in that you carve away the areas you don't want to print, but it carves so easily it's a joy to work with. Once you have your design carved out you can attach it to a wooden or acrylic block if necessary, to give it more structure. You load your stamp with paint using a sponge and print onto fabric by applying even pressure to the back. These blocks will last as long as you look after the rubber, so you can use them again and again. As with the lino, take great care when carving because the tools are very sharp.

Tools—Erasers, rubber carving block, lino cutters, sharp knife, wooden or acrylic backing blocks, sponge roller, clean roller/brayer.

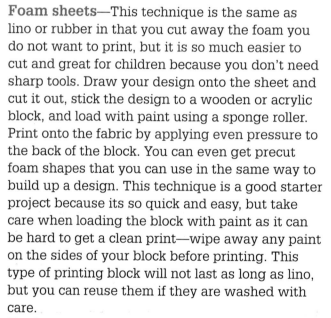

Foam sheets

Polystyrene tile

Foam sheets—This technique is the same as lino or rubber in that you cut away the foam you do not want to print, but it is so much easier to cut and great for children because you don't need sharp tools. Draw your design onto the sheet and cut it out, stick the design to a wooden or acrylic block, and load with paint using a sponge roller. Print onto the fabric by applying even pressure to the back of the block. You can even get precut foam shapes that you can use in the same way to build up a design. This technique is a good starter project because its so quick and easy, but take care when loading the block with paint as it can be hard to get a clean print—wipe away any paint on the sides of your block before printing. This type of printing block will not last as long as lino, but you can reuse them if they are washed with care.

Tools—Foam craft sheets or precut shapes, scissors, glue, wooden or acrylic backing block, sponge roller, clean roller/brayer.

Polystyrene tile—Again, you may have memories of printing with polystyrene tiles at school. It is a simple technique where you push into the tile surface creating areas where the paint cannot load and these will be the blank areas of your print. Use a pen or blunt pencil to make your marks. Once your design is complete, load the paint onto the tile with a sponge roller and print by applying even pressure to the back of the tile, either with a clean brayer or your hands. This printing block is only good for a few projects because it is hard to keep the sheet undamaged. You could stick it to a firm backing if you wanted to preserve it for longer. Take care not to go through to the back when you are scoring your tile.

Tools—Polystyrene tile, pen, scissors, sponge roller, clean roller/brayer.

Resist printing

Resist printing describes where a stencil or coating is used to resist the paint, allowing paint through only certain areas and onto the fabric.

Stencil—A stencil can be as simple or as complicated as you like—all you need to be aware of is that your image is cut out as one continuous piece leaving behind the stencil that will mask the fabric from the paint. You can use thin card or acetate to make your stencil. Another good option is freezer paper or butchers' paper because it is waterproof and has a plastic backing which, when ironed, sticks to the fabric temporarily giving you a crisp clean edge to your print. You can also use contact paper, which has a peal off sticky back. Stencils only have a limited life, but freezer paper and acetate will be reusable a few times. Once you have cut your stencil and placed it on the fabric, use a stencil brush, roller, or sponge roller to lightly apply the paint; build it up in layers because too much paint will bleed under the stencil. Always use a sharp new craft blade to cut out your stencil and take great care.
Tools—Paper, acetate or freezer paper, sharp craft knife, sponge, stencil brush, clean roller/brayer.

Stencil

Stencil screen print—Screen printing gives a very professional finish to your design. It applies an even, thin coat of paint to the surface of the fabric. You will need to cut out a stencil and secure it to the back of the screen using masking tape, leaving no gaps at the edges of the stencil where the paint could come through. Place the screen onto the fabric and pull the paint across the surface of the screen with a squeegee, holding the screen steady as you do so. Make sure you clean your screens well and never allow paint to dry on them. Your blank screen will last for hundreds of prints but you will need to prepare a new stencil for each new project.
Tools—Silk screen, squeegee, masking tape, stencil paper, sharp craft knife.

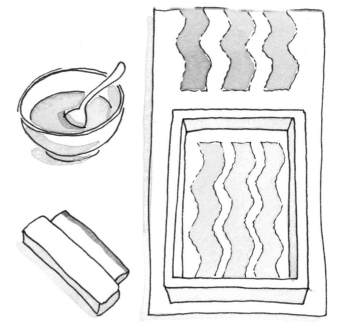

Stencil screen print

Other printing methods

There are many ways to make marks and transfer images to a surface. Here are the ones used in this book.

Leaf print—This is so simple and yet it can lead to designs you'd never expect. Simply roller the paint onto the back of a leaf and place it on the fabric, use a clean roller to press, and carefully peal off the leaf. Depending on how delicate the leaf is you can get a few prints from one leaf. Let the garden inspire you and try out different things.

Tools—Leaves, sponge roller, clean roller/brayer.

Leaf print

Photo transfer—Photo transfer is a digital printing technique using an inkjet printer and specialist iron-on transfer paper. For the projects in this book, you will need to scan the images on page 126 into your computer. You can also make your image on the computer, it could be a simple photograph, a scan of a child's drawing, or a layered image made in an art program. Once you have created your artwork you must reverse it because the print will go on face down—choose flip, reverse, or similar command within your picture-editing program. Print out your image onto the photo-transfer paper, trim it so that there is just a small border, and iron it onto the fabric in accordance with the manufacturer's instructions. Once it has cooled you can peel away the backing paper and you are left with your image on the fabric. You must take care not to iron directly onto the transfer and wash inside out—with care this can be quite a durable print.

Tools—Computer, inkjet printer, photo-transfer paper.

Photo transfer

Sun print (cyanotype)

Sun print (cyanotype)—This is a photographic printing technique were fabric is sensitized to sunlight with mild chemicals, then objects are placed onto the fabric and left to develop in the sun. Cyanotype kits are readily available and the chemicals, although they should always be treated with care, are not as scary as they may sound. You can also buy ready sensitized fabric or milder sun sensitive paint if you prefer. Always follow the instructions carefully, but the basic method is to mix up your photosensitive solution and paint it onto the fabric in a darkened environment. Allow the fabric to dry in the dark and once it is completely dry you can lay your design elements on top; this could be leaves, a design cut out with scissors, or, as in the project on page 100, a lace curtain. Place the fabric and layers in the sun and the paint will change to a dark green color when it is done. Remove the objects and wash in cold water, the blue color will start to develop and the white areas will become clearer. It's an exciting process, but may be worth a few tests first until you get the image you are after.
Tools—Cyanotype kit, objects to create design with, the sun!

Printing essentials—10 top tips

1 Do a test print! Always—no matter how confident you are—try out your print on some scrap fabric first, it will help you to get your final project perfect first time.

2 It's always best to use a small sponge or brush to apply the paint to potato prints to get a smoother covering.

3 Use baby wipes or a clean wet rag to clean off the edges of printing blocks after loading with paint, this will help to prevent many imperfections.

4 Try layering a few different printing techniques together—see the Wine gift bag project (page 84) where large stencils were combined with rubber stamps to create the design.

5 Always make sure the paint is dry in between layers or it will bleed and smudge—and always print your background first, if you have one. A hair dryer is a useful addition to your working space to dry layers between prints.

6 Don't allow fabric paint to dry on your printing block as it will ruin it and it won't be usable again.

7 Always set your dried print by ironing with a hot iron; this will make it waterproof and give a clean, crisp finish.

8 If a print design is complicated—or if it is a geometric design that needs to be straight or aligned—it's a great idea to mark where you want your pattern to be on the fabric before you start to print. You can do this with a pencil or chalk.

9 If your design calls for simple stripes, as in the Shaped tote bag, page 80, then you could use masking tape to mask off the areas you don't want to print.

10 When working with text always remember to reverse your design!

print motifs

All of these templates, unless otherwise stated, are printed at half their actual size. They will need to be enlarged to 200%—using a photocopier—before use.

Metal-frame coin purse—leaves and butterflies, page 38

Drawstring pouch—swallows, page 40

Toiletry bag—roses and leaf, page 52

Kids' messenger bag—video game, page 43

Roll storage—cutlery, page 92

Book bag—crayons, page 46

Triangle coin purse—
teardrops, page 22
(actual size)

Children's
backback—sea,
boat, and seagulls,
page 36

Metal frame handbag—seed
heads, page 24

Bucket storage bags—grasses and bird,
page 102

Wine gift bag—large
flowers, page 94
(enlarge to four times
this size—400%)

Rounded shoulder bag—bird on branch, page 98

Lunch bag—bottles, page 66

Shaped tote bag—succulents, page 90

Jeans bag—stag, page 48

Slouchy shoulder bag—leaves, page 72

Bucket handled bag—
ginkgo, page 26

Envelope clutch—feathers, page 30

Gathered handbag—damask, page 82

Men's messenger bag—mustaches, page 96

Long satchel—daisy, page 33

Small shoulder pouch – stems, page 28 (enlarge to four times this size—400%)

Boxy weekender—large foliage, page 84

CHAPTER 1

carved block printing

In this section you will learn all about carving your own printing
blocks using lino sheets, rubber blocks, and erasers. The technique
is very simple—you carve away parts of the block to create
your designs.

triangle coin purse

This purse is cute, kooky, and easy to make; allow yourself to be inspired and develop the idea. The print is made up of very simple teardrop and spot shapes made from a carved eraser, so it's easy to do and always effective.

Print TEARDROPS ERASER STAMP

skill level

materials

Motif on page 17

Main fabric: cut two, 7 x 5½in (18 x 14.5cm)

Lining fabric: cut two, 7 x 5½in (18 x 14.5cm)

Iron-on interfacing: cut two, 7 x 5½in (18 x 14.5cm)

Handle strip: cut one, 10 x 2in (25 x 5cm)

Matching zipper, 7in (18cm)

Matching thread

Two new, flat surfaced erasers

Lino cutter

Sharp knife

Fabric paint

Sponge

Soft paintbrush

1 Prepare your carved eraser stamps as described on page 11. Cut a teardrop using the motif on page 17, and make a simple, round shape from the second eraser. Then, cut your fabric pieces to shape and print your fabric. Once the design is dry, iron it to set the fabric paint. To stiffen the main fabric, iron on the interfacing.

2 Make up the handle strip by pressing ¼in (6mm) edges along its length, fold in half to match the edges. Topstitch (over sew) the seams on both sides.

3 Sew the zipper to the main fabric pieces on the 7in (18cm) sides—right side of fabric to right side of zipper. Then sew the lining to the zipper following the same line of stitching, press, and topstitch (over sew) along the zipper edge for a neat finish. Make sure that both the lining and main fabrics are laying flat.

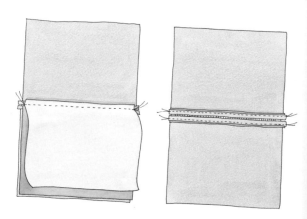

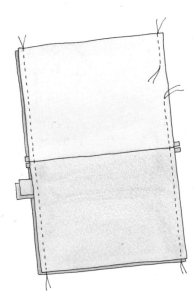

4 Open the fabric out and match up the lining fabric and the main fabric with right sides together. Pin the folded handle strip in between the main fabric layers facing inward and sew the side seams, enclosing the zipper and leaving a small opening in one side seam of the lining fabric.

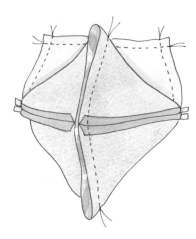

5 On the main fabric, pinch together the bottom so that the side seams line up creating a triangle shape; sew a ⅜in (1cm) closing seam.

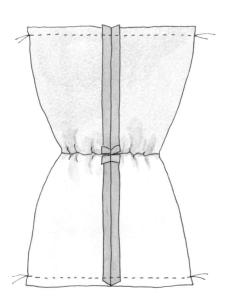

6 Repeat step 5 with the lining fabric.

7 Turn the whole purse right side out. Reach through the opening in the lining to form the triangle shape and press. Close the opening in the lining fabric either by hand stitching or by machine.

metal-frame bag

You will find many different shaped frames are available, but the principle for making a bag with them is the same whatever the shape: a simple pouch bag with a channel at the top edge that you use to attach it to the frame. An arched frame is used here and the fabric is printed with a repeat pattern made using a simple stamp, and using two color shades.

print SEED HEADS RUBBER STAMP   *skill level*

1 Cut out your fabric slightly larger than your pattern pieces and iron it. Using the print motifs on page 17, prepare your carved rubber blocks as described on page 11 and print your design on the fabric. Once you are finished, allow the fabric to dry completely before ironing to set the paint.

materials
Motifs on page 17

Template on page 119

Main fabric: cut two on fold, 16 x 14in (41 x 36cm)

Lining fabric: cut two on fold, 16 x 14in (41 x 36cm)

12in (30cm) diameter metal handles

Matching thread

2 x 4in (10cm) square rubber sheets

Lino cutting tools

Sharp knife

Fabric paint

Sponge roller

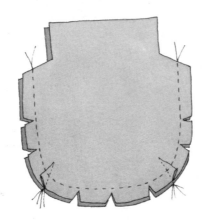

2 Using the pattern template from page 119, cut your fabric to size accurately and mark the position of the darts on the wrong side of the fabric. Sew closed the darts on all four fabric pieces using a ⅜in (1cm) seam allowance. Then, working with the main fabric pieces, place them right sides facing together and sew around the curved sides and base with a ⅜in (1cm) seam. Clip the curves.

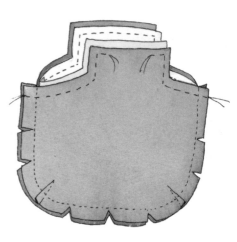

3 Sew the lining in the same way as the main fabric in step 2. To attach the lining to the main fabric, leave the main fabric inside out, but turn the lining fabric wrong side out and insert it into the main bag pouch, pin, then sew closed with a ⅜in (1cm) seam around the top edge and side openings. Leave a small gap on one side to allow turning.

4 Pull the bag through the opening in the lining and turn it right side out. Press the top seam opening closed. Fold over the top edge inside the bag by ¾in (2cm), pin in place, and sew a neat seam closing the opening in the lining, and creating a channel to feed the handle frame through. Repeat on the other side of the bag.

5 Undo the end screw of the frame (check the instructions that came with your frame), thread the bar through the channel, and reattach the end screws holding the handle in place.

bucket handled bag

The stand-alone structure of this unusually shaped bag makes
it ideal for transporting your craft projects when you're on the go.
You could glam it up with a satin lining or use a color
to match your décor.

print GINKGO STEMS, LINO PRINT

skill level

materials

Motif on page 18

Template on page 124

Main fabric: cut one on
fold, 14½ x 17in
(37 x 43cm)

Lining fabric: cut one on
fold, 14½ x 17in
(37 x 43cm)

Iron-on interfacing: cut
one on fold, 14½ x 17in
(37 x 43cm)

Matching thread

Lino sheet

Lino cutters

Fabric paint

1 Prepare your lino block as described on
page 11. Then, cut out the main fabric
slightly larger than needed. Mark out your
pattern shape in dressmakers' chalk or pencil,
so that it is easier to place your design. Due
to the structure of this bag, there is a 2in
(5cm) area at each end of the fabric that you
should keep free of your print because this
will become the base of the bag. Print your
design onto the fabric. When the print is dry,
iron it to set the fabric paint.

2 Using the pattern template on page 124,
cut your main fabric to size and cut out
the lining fabric piece. To stiffen your main
fabric, iron on the interfacing.

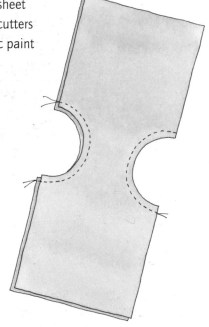

3 With right sides
together, pin and sew
the main fabric and lining
fabric together around the
handle hole taking a ⅜in
(1cm) seam.

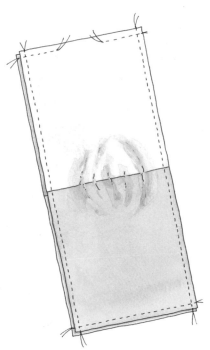

4 Snip around the inside
curves and turn right
side out. Press the sewn
handle section. Now open
out the main bag parts of
the fabric and, with the
right sides together, and
temporarily enclosing the
handle part of the bag,
sew the side seams of the
main fabric.

5 Repeat the same process on the other
side with the lining fabric side seams.
Now sew closed the main fabric bottom
seam, and sew the lining fabric bottom seam
leaving a small gap in the center for turning.

6 On the main fabric piece, turn and fold the fabric so that the bottom of the bag is flattened, the seam is in the center, and two protruding corner triangles are created. Sew a closing seam 1½in (4cm) in from each corner.

7 Repeat the same process with the lining fabric to flatten the bottom of the bag, and then turn the whole bag right side out through the opening in the lining.

8 Press the seams around the handle and topstitch (over sew) around the bag opening. Close the opening in the lining, either by hand or machine.

small shoulder pouch

This simple pouch design is based around an A4 (11¾ x 8¼ in /297 x 210 mm) paper pattern. It's simple to make and ideal for using up a leftover piece of fabric; the delicate print complements its simple style. You could use any of the print designs in the book to create your own style.

print STEMS ERASER STAMP   **skill level**

materials

Motif on page 19

Main fabric

Main panel: cut two, 10 x 8in (25 x 20cm)

Pocket piece: cut one, 8 x 6in (20 x 16cm)

Handle strip: cut one, 47 x 3in (120 x 8cm)

Lining fabric

Main panel: cut two, 10 x 8in (25 x 20cm)

Pocket piece: cut one, 8 x 6in (20 x 16cm)

Self-cover button, 1in (25mm) diameter

Elastic cord: 6in (15cm)

Matching thread

Large, long eraser

Lino cutters

Sharp knife

Sponge roller

Fabric paint

1 Prepare your eraser printing block as described on page 11. Then, cut your pattern pieces out of your main and lining fabrics, and print your design onto the front piece of the main fabric. Once it is dry, iron it to set the fabric paint.

2 To create the strap, press ¼ in (6mm) seams on each side of the fabric, fold, and press to match up the side seams. Sew all along both sides to finish.

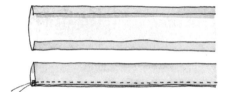

3 With right sides together, sew the pocket pieces together with a ⅜in (1cm) seam, press, and turn right sides out. Topstitch (over sew) the top edge.

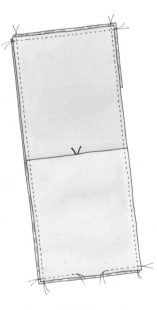

4 Pin the loop of elastic in place, facing downward, on the top edge of the back main fabric. With right sides together, sew the main and lining fabrics together with a ⅜in (1cm) seam to close the top edge, catching the elastic in the seam. Sew the top seam of the front pieces together in the same way. Press the seams.

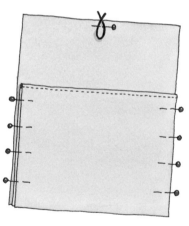

5 Pin the pocket piece in place on the right side of the main fabric. Open out the main bag pieces and, with right sides together, match the main fabric and lining fabric so that they are laying on top of each other. Pin and then sew around the entire outer edge with a ⅜in (1cm) seam, catching the pocket piece, and leaving a small opening at the base for turning.

6 Trim all corners and turn right side out. Press and topstitch (over sew) the top edge seam of the bag. Pin the handles in place at the sides of the bag on the outside, folding under the raw edge and, making sure the lining is laying flat inside the bag, sew a square of stitches to secure the handles in place.

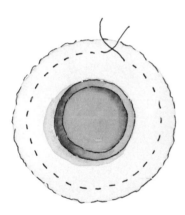

7 To cover your button, cut a circle of main fabric about ⅜in (1cm) bigger than the button. Using a needle and strong thread, sew a rough running stitch all around the circle about ¼in (6mm) in from the edge. Place the fabric over the button and pull the running stitch to gather the fabric tightly around the button. Holding the gathered thread tight, press the back of the button on, it will snap into place holding the fabric permanently around the button. Sew in place on the front of the bag to correspond with the loop of elastic

envelope clutch

This stylish clutch is perfect for an evening out, wedding, or a glamorous event. It's a practical size to hold all the essentials, and has an eye-catching design. This is an easy pattern to make up, using only a rectangle and a triangle of fabric.

print FEATHERS, LINO PRINT

skill level

materials

Motif on page 18

Main fabric

Main piece: cut one, 17½ x 12½in (44 x 32cm)

Flap piece: cut one, 12½ x 9½in (32 x 24cm)

Lining fabric

Main piece: cut one, 17½ x 12½in (44 x 32cm)

Flap piece: cut one, 12½ x 9½in (32 x 24cm)

Iron-on interfacing

Main piece: cut one, 17½ x 12½in (44 x 32cm)

Flap piece: cut one, 12½ x 9½in (32 x 24cm)

Magnetic bag clasp

Matching thread

Lino sheet

Lino cutters

Fabric paint

Sponge roller

1 Prepare your lino blocks as described on page 11. Then, cut out the pieces of your main fabric slightly larger than your actual pattern pieces, mark where you want the print in chalk or pencil, and print your design onto the fabric. Once it's dry, iron it to set the fabric paint. Now you can accurately cut out your pattern pieces in all fabrics.

2 On both the main and the lining fabrics, working on the wrong side, find and mark the center of the main piece with a line of chalk or pencil. Measure 2½in (6cm) from the top edge on both long sides and mark. Draw a connecting, diagonal line from the side mark to the center at the end and cut on this line. Iron the interfacing onto all the main fabric pieces.

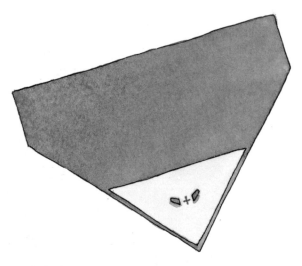

3 To attach the magnetic clasp, work first with the top part of the clasp (the thinner part). On the lining fabric flap piece, iron on a small piece of interfacing, to cover and strengthen the triangle point, to about 4in (10cm) high. Measure up 2½in (6cm) from the point and mark, measure in 2in (5cm) from both sides to meet your first measurement and mark. On the right side of the fabric, cut two small slits next to the mark and push the fixing arms of the clasp through the fabric. On the wrong side of the fabric, fold the fixing arms over each other to secure in place.

4 With right sides together, sew the main fabric and lining flap pieces together with a ⅜in (1cm) seam. Trim the corners, turn right side out, and press. Topstitch (over sew) a neat line of stitches to finish the edge off. Press and baste (tack) or pin the top edge of the flap to create a neat finished edge. Take the flap piece and pin it to the right side of the main fabric piece about 2½in (6cm) from the top edge, sew in place with a neat seam that both closes the flap edge and attaches it to the bag at the same time.

5 To mark where the magnetic clasp is going to go, fold the bag into its finished shape, fold the top flap over onto the outside of the main fabric and mark where the closing part of the fixing should go.

6 Open out the bag again and attach the second part of the fixing where you made a mark in step 5.

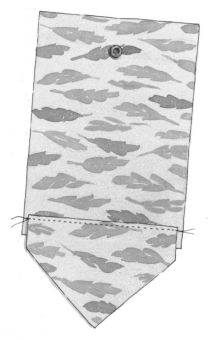

7 Sew ⅜in (1cm) side seams of the main and lining fabric pieces. Turn only the lining right side out and insert it into the bag pouch. Sew a ⅜in (1cm) top edge seam, leaving a small opening at the back to allow for turning.

8 Turn right side out, press the top edge, and topstitch (over sew) to close the opening and finish off the bag.

long satchel

This is a flat, body-hugging shoulder bag, big enough to fit all your essentials inside. A secure zippered main bag and easy-access front pockets make this a great bag to take out and about. The bag is printed with a fun daisy design.

Print DAISIES, ERASER STAMP

skill level

1 Cut out your main fabric slightly larger than the pattern pieces and press ready for printing. Prepare your eraser stamp as described on page 11 and print your fabric. Once the print has dried, iron the fabric at a high heat to set the fabric paint. Cut out your pattern pieces accurately and iron the interfacing onto the main fabric.

2 Take the front pocket pieces and, with right sides together (main and lining fabrics), sew a ⅜in (1cm) seam along the top edge, turn right side out, press, and topstitch (over sew). Place the made up pocket onto the right side of the main front fabric piece and sew with a dividing seam creating two front pockets.

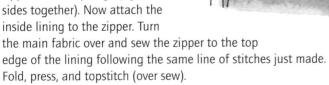

3 Working with the fabric front piece that you have just attached the pocket to, place the zipper face down on the right side of the fabric and sew the zipper to the top edge (right sides together). Now attach the inside lining to the zipper. Turn the main fabric over and sew the zipper to the top edge of the lining following the same line of stitches just made. Fold, press, and topstitch (over sew).

materials

Motifs on page 19

Main fabric

Bottom front: cut one, 11 x 13in (28 x 33cm)

Top front: cut one, 11 x 2½in (28 x 6cm)

Front pocket: cut one, 11 x 9in (28 x 23cm)

Back: cut one, 11 x 15in (28 x 38cm)

Lining fabric

Bottom front: cut one, 11 x 13in (28 x 33cm)

Front pocket: cut one, 11 x 9in (28 x 23cm)

Back: cut one, 11 x 15in (28 x 38cm)

Iron-on interfacing

Back: cut one, 11 x 15in (28 x 38cm)

Matching zipper, 12in (30cm)

Matching thread

Two eyelets—large enough to work with the trigger hooks

Two trigger hooks (dog leash clips)

Cotton tape, approx. 39in (1m)

Rubber sheet or large eraser

Lino cutting tools

Fabric paint

Sponge roller

4 Sew the other side of the zipper to the small front top section of the main front piece of fabric. Lay the top fabric section facedown over the front of the zipper and sew along the zipper edge, fold the main fabric away from the zipper, and press. Lay the whole front section on the right side of the central lining and sew together with a line of stitches along the top edge of the zipper.

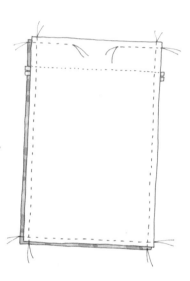

5 You can now attach the back panel to complete the bag. Place the constructed front section, right sides facing together, onto the main fabric back piece, pin, and sew a ⅜in (1cm) seam around the whole bag, leaving a small opening at the top for turning.

6 Trim the corners and turn the whole bag right side out. Flatten the bag, press, and topstitch (over sew) a neat seam around the top part of the bag. Attach eyelets in each corner.

7 Cotton tape and trigger hooks are used to make the handles. Cut the strap to length, allowing an extra 4in (10cm) at each end to thread through the trigger hooks. Fold the strap back on itself at each end and sew in place with a square of stitches. Attach to the bag with the trigger hooks.

children's backpack

This useful little backpack is great for carrying school sports kit, a day at the beach, or an after-school activity. The print design used here is a nautical scene built up with three different pictorial elements.

print WAVES, BOATS, AND GULLS, LINO

skill level

1 Prepare your lino as described on page 11. Cut out your fabric and press it ready to print. Apply the print. Once your print is dry, iron your fabric at a high temperature to set the fabric paint.

2 To make the tabs for the cord to be threaded through, take your strips of fabric, fold in half, then press a ⅜in (1cm) hem on both edges. Fold in the middle so that the edges meet up and topstitch (over sew) down both edges to finish. Make up two tabs.

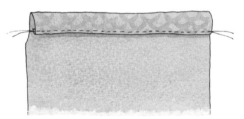

materials

Motifs on page 17

Main fabric

Main panel: cut two, 14 x 16½in (35 x 42cm)

Cord tabs: cut two, 2 x 3in (5 x 8cm)

Matching thread

Cord, approx. 79in (2m)

Lino sheet

Lino cutters

Fabric paint

Sponge roller

3 Prepare the top edges of the bag to make neat openings for the cord handles. Make a snip approximately ⅜in (1cm) into the side edges, 2in (5cm) down from the top edge on both sides. Fold over, press, and sew a ⅜in (1cm) seam on both sides.

4 To make the channel through which the cord handles will be threaded, fold over and press a ⅜in (1cm) hem along the whole top edge, and then fold again, press, and sew a ¾in (2cm) hem creating a channel along the top edge. Do this on both pieces of fabric.

5 French seams are used to make up the bag. Take the two main pieces of fabric and place them wrong sides together. Pin the cord tabs that you made in step 2, 2in (5cm) up from the bottom of the bag, facing inward toward the center of the bag and sew a ⅜in (1cm) seam around the two sides and bottom.

6 Trim the seam edges down so that they are as narrow as you can make them without compromising the stitches. Turn inside out and press the seams. Sew another ⅜in (1cm) seam down the sides enclosing all the raw edges inside and securing the tabs on each side. Turn right side out and press.

7 To thread the handle cord to the bag, attach a safety pin to one end of the cord to help you to guide it through the channels. Start by threading one end of the cord around the top of the bag and out of the same side hole it went into. Run the cord right down to the tab at the bottom and thread one end through the tab, then tie the two ends together. Repeat on the other side of the bag in the same way. Now, when you pull the handles they will open and close the bag top.

metal-frame coin purse

Purse frames come in all sorts of shapes and sizes; all easily available from crafts stores. This cute little coin purse has a vintage feel to it; the fabric is printed with carved eraser stamps using a delicate leaf and vine design and a few butterflies fluttering by.

print LEAVES AND BUTTERFLIES, ERASER STAMP *skill level*

1 Prepare your carved eraser stamp as described on page 11 and cut out your fabric slightly larger than your pattern pieces to make the printing easier. Then, print your fabric. Allow the fabric to dry and then iron it at a high heat to set the fabric paint. Using the pattern template from page 118, cut your fabric to size accurately, and mark the positions of the darts on the wrong side of the fabric.

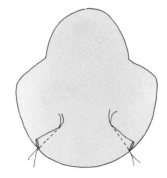

2 Sew the darts on all four pieces of fabric, main and lining, with a ⅜in (1cm) seam allowance. Lay the fabric flat and press the seams.

materials

Motifs on page 16

Template on page 118

Main fabric: cut two, 9 x 9in (23 x 23cm)

Lining fabric: cut two, 9 x 9in (23 x 23cm)

Matching thread

Three large erasers or one small sheet of rubber block

Lino carving tools

Sharp knife

Fabric paints

Sponges

Metal purse frame—this pattern calls for a 3in (8cm) frame

Strong glue

3 With right sides together, and ensuring that the darts match up, sew the two main fabric pieces together, following the edge around the bottom of the purse with a ⅜in (1cm) seam—don't sew the top portion of the purse, this will be attached to the frame at the opening. Clip the curves.

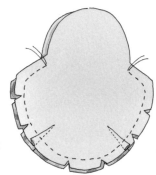

4 Sew the lining fabric pieces together in the same way as you did the main fabric, but leave a 4in (10cm) gap at the bottom for turning. Now sew the main and lining fabrics together. Leave the main fabric pouch inside out and turn the lining pouch right side out. Insert the lining into the main pouch and sew a ⅜in (1cm) seam around both top edges. Clip the curves.

5 Turn the whole purse right side out through the opening in the lining. Push out the top seams so that they lay smooth and flat, press the top edges, and sew the opening in the lining closed.

6 The purse is attached to the metal frame with glue. Put a line of glue along the top edge of the purse and carefully push the bag edge into channel. Use a seam ripper or another pointed tool to poke the fabric into place. Leave to dry, and then attach the other side. Clean off any excess glue while it is still wet.

drawstring pouch

This little bag has a very timeless feel to it. It can be a very pretty bag if made with delicate fabrics and soft prints, or a cool pirate's treasure bag if made with bold colors and skull prints—you decide. The print used here is of swifts and swallows.

print SWIFTS AND SWALLOWS, ERASER STAMP *skill level*

materials

Motifs on page 16

Main fabric

Sides: cut four, 4 x 6in (10 x 15cm)

Base: cut one, 4 x 4in (10 x 10cm)

Lining fabric

Sides: cut four, 4 x 6in (10 x 15cm)

Base: cut one, 4 x 4in (10 x 10cm)

Iron-on interfacing

Base: cut one, 4 x 4in (10 x 10cm)

Matching thread

Satin cord (for the handle), approx. 39in (1m)

Thin satin cord (for the drawstring), approx. 39in (1m)

Several large erasers

Lino cutting tools

Fabric paint

Sponges

1 Cut out a large piece of fabric measuring 22 x 8in (55 x 20cm)—you will use this to cut out your pattern pieces after printing. Prepare your eraser stamps as described on page 11. Once you have built up your design, allow it to dry fully before ironing at a high temperature to set the paint.

2 Cut out all of the pattern pieces and iron interfacing onto the main fabric base piece.

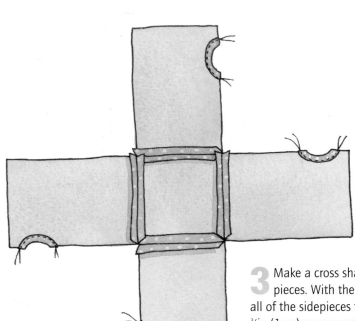

3 Make a cross shape with all the fabric pieces. With the right sides together, sew all of the sidepieces to the base piece using ⅜in (1cm) seams and leaving ⅜in (1cm) gaps at each end. To make a channel for the drawstring to come through, snip into the edge of the fabric ¾in (2cm) down from the top edges, and again a further 1in (2.5cm) down. Turn in a 3/8in (1cm) hem, repeat on all sidepieces so that they will line up when the sides are sewn up. They need to be placed opposite one another on adjacent side panels.

4 Sew the sides using ⅜in (1cm) seams and making sure to leave the drawstring channels open. Sew the lining in the same way but without the need for the drawstring channel holes.

5 The bag is made up using the "pull-through" method. With the main fabric still inside out, turn the lining fabric pouch right sides facing out and insert it into the main bag pouch. Pin the handle cord in place in opposite corners, facing down and positioned next to the drawstring channel holes. Sew around the top edge of the bag (including the handle cord) using a ⅜in (1cm) seam and leaving a small opening for turning right side out—reverse stitch a few times over the handles for extra security.

6 Turn the whole bag right side out by pulling it through the opening and press the top edge. Sew around the top edge with a neat seam closing the opening and finishing off the top. To create the channel for the drawstring, sew around the whole bag ½in (1.5cm) down from the top edge then sew another seam all the way around 1½in (4cm) from the top edge. Take care to ensure that the lining is laying flat inside the bag as you do this.

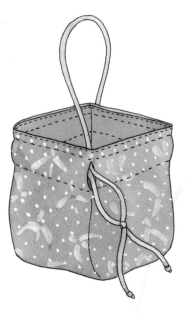

7 To thread the drawstring cords through the channels, use a closed safety pin attached to one end to guide it. Thread one cord in the right-side hole, all around the bag, and out of the right side hole. Thread the other cord in the left-side hole, all the way around, and out of the left-side hole. Cut the cords to the desired length and tie together with a knot to secure.

kids' messenger bag

This is a practical and funky little bag with a video game print—the spaceship pattern is built up with a single, small square stamp. The bag is perfect for school, with space for school supplies.

Print VIDEO GAME, ERASER STAMP

skill level

1 Cut out your pattern pieces and prepare a small, square eraser stamp as described on page 11. Mark out your design in chalk first, using the motifs on page 16 as a guide, and then build up your image, one square at a time. Once it's dry, iron it to set the fabric paint.

2 Iron the interfacing onto the main fabric, and then make up the smaller elements first. To make the strap, fold and press ⅜in (1cm) hems on both sides of the handle strip, fold and press the strip in half, and sew a neat edge seam down both sides of the handle to finish. Now make up the flap—with the right sides together (main fabric and lining) sew the flap pieces together with a ⅜in (1cm) seam leaving the top open. Snip the corners, turn right side out, and press. Topstitch (over sew) a neat edge on the sides and bottom edge to finish.

materials

Motifs on page 16

Main fabric

Body of bag: cut one, 19 x 7in (48 x 18cm)

Flap: cut one, 9 x 8in (24 x 20cm)

Handle strip: cut one, 2 x 31½in (6 x 80cm)

Lining fabric

Body of bag: cut one, 19 x 7in (48 x 18cm)

Flap: cut one, 9 x 8in (24 x 20cm)

Iron-on interfacing

Body of bag: cut one, 19 x 7in (48 x 18cm)

Flap: cut one, 9 x 8in (24 x 20cm)

Matching thread

Small eraser

Sharp knife

Fabric paint

Sponge

3 To construct the main bag pouch, with the right side facing inward, using a ⅜in (1cm) seam, sew the back seam of the main fabric piece closed. Press so that the seam is in the center and sew the bottom seam closed.

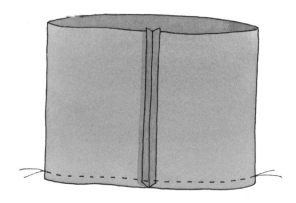

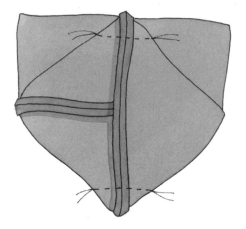

4 To make the bottom of the bag flat, fold out the bag so that the bottom of the bag is flattened, the seam is in the center, and two protruding corner triangles are created. Press the fold and sew a closing seam 2in (5cm) in from each corner, trim the corners off, and turn right side out. Make up the lining pouch in exactly the same way.

5 Leave the lining pouch right side facing inward and insert it into the main bag pouch. On both the main and lining fabrics fold the top edges over by ⅜in (1cm) and press. You can now attach the handles and flap in one go. Pin the handles in place on either side of the bag, pin the flap in place to the back of the bag, and pin the lining in place around the whole top edge of the bag. Sew a neat seam all around the top edge, closing the top edge and capturing the handles and flap.

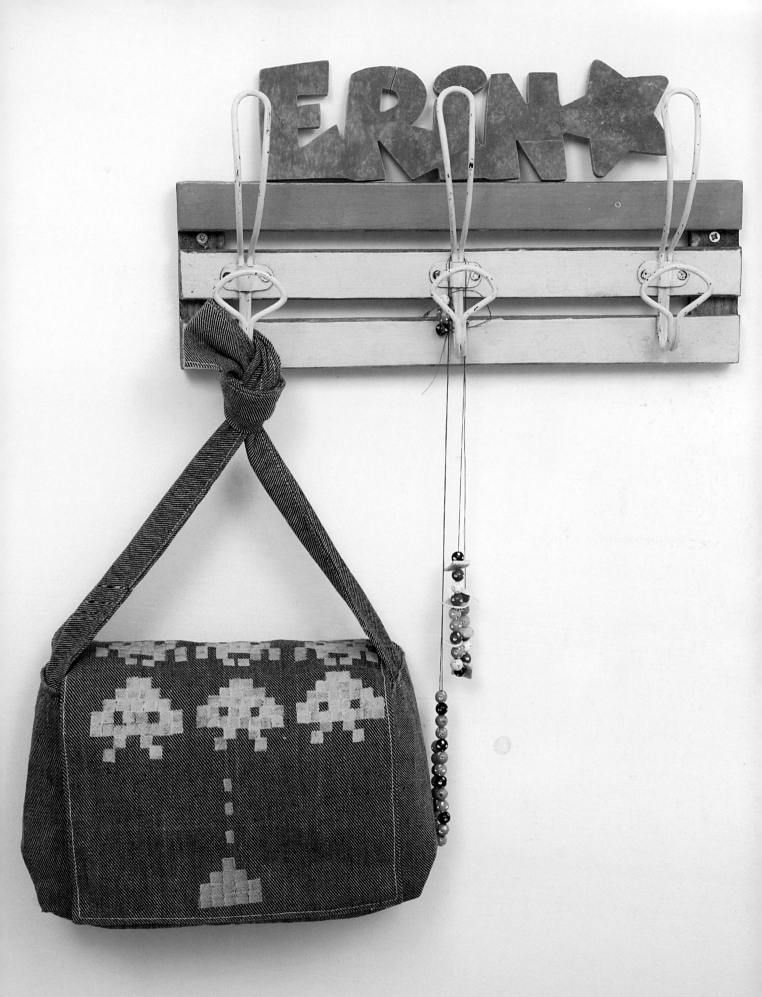

book bag

This easy pattern is based on the classic school bag that so many children have when they start school, it's great for carrying around their music books, textbooks or artwork. You can make it as funky or a plain as you like with your print design.

print CRAYONS, ERASER STAMP

skill level

materials

Motifs on page 17

Main fabric

Back piece: cut one,
  20 x 16in (50 x 40cm)

Front piece: cut one,
  16 x 12in (40 x 30cm)

Lining fabric

Back piece: cut one,
  20 x 16in (50 x 40cm)

Front piece: cut one,
  16 x 12in (40 x 30cm)

Iron-on interfacing

Back piece: cut one,
  20 x 16in (50 x 40cm)

Front piece: cut one,
  16 x 12in (40 x 30cm)

Matching thread

Elastic

2 large buttons

Cotton tape, approx.
  10in (25cm)

Large eraser or rubber
  block

Lino carving tools

Fabric paint

Sponge

1 Cut out your pattern pieces accurately before printing with this project. To taper the flap edges, take your larger back fabric pieces (main and lining); find the center of the top edge, and mark 6in (15cm) either side of it so that you have a 12in (30cm) section marked. On both side edges, measure 4in (10cm) down and mark. Draw lines connecting the edges to the 12in (30cm) section on both sides, and cut off the corners.

2 Prepare your eraser stamp as described on page 11 and apply the print. Allow the print to dry fully before ironing at a high heat to set the fabric paint.

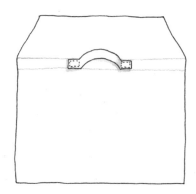

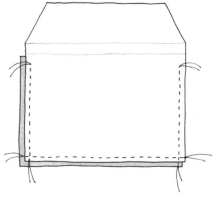

3 Iron the interfacing onto the main fabric. To attach the cotton tape handle, on the main fabric back piece, fold along the line where the piece starts to taper and press to make a crease, then fold 1in (2.5cm) down from the first fold and press to make another crease. Pin and sew the cotton tape handle in place in the center.

4 With right sides together, sew the two main fabric pieces together using a ⅜in (1cm) seam and leaving a ¾in (2cm gap) at the top of each side seam.

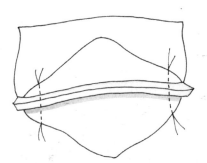

5 To make the bottom of the bag flat, fold out the bag so that the bottom is flattened, the seam is in the center, and two protruding corner triangles are created. Press the fold, sew a closing seam 1½in (4cm) in from each corner, and trim the corners off.

6 Make up the lining in the same way as you did the main bag, but without the handle.

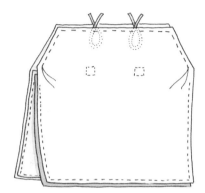

7 On the front flap of the main bag, on the right side of the fabric, pin two elastic loops in place pointing down toward the bag. To attach the lining to the main bag, place the right sides of the main and lining fabric together, pin, and sew a ⅜in (1cm) seam around the top flap edges, making sure to capture the elastic loops.

8 Trim the corners and turn the whole bag right side out. Push the lining inside the main bag pouch, press the top flap and the front top edge, and topstitch (over sew) around the flap and opening to finish. Sew the buttons on the front of the bag.

jeans bag

This is a great way of recycling an old pair of ripped jeans. Kids' jeans were used here to make a small bag but a big baggy pair of men's jeans would make a great traveling bag. There is a print on the lining fabric as well as on the outside, for an extra treat!

---

print STAG HEAD, LINO

skill level

materials

Motif on page 18

Old pair of jeans

Lining fabric: cut to the size of the jean bag

Matching thread

Lino sheet

Lino cutters

Sponge roller

Fabric paint

1 Prepare your lino print as described on page 11.

2 To prepare the pair of jeans before printing, cut off the legs about 4in (10cm) down from the crotch. Watch out for the back pockets, if they are placed lower, you will have to cut lower. Carefully unpick the inner leg seams until the fabric is laying flat across itself. Pin and stitch the leg fabric flat following the line of the original stitches to make one flat piece front and back.

3 You can now print the jeans fabric. Make sure to find a flat surface or your print will be imperfect—the end of an ironing board works well. Push the jeans over the end of the ironing board and make sure the inside pockets are tucked out of the way and print. Once the print is dry, iron the jeans on a high setting to set the fabric paint.

4 To make the jeans into a bag, turn them inside out and sew the base seam of the jeans closed. Turn right side out again and press the bottom edge.

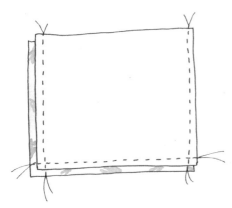

5 To make your lining, trace around the bag shape you have made and cut out two pieces of fabric to this pattern allowing a ⅜in (1cm) seam allowance. The lining fabric is printed with the same design, as the jeans, randomly placed all over the fabric. Make sure to iron the lining on a high heat to set the paint before sewing. Sew the side and base seams of the lining, fold the top edge toward the outside, and press a ⅜in (1cm) hem around the top. Insert the lining into the main jeans bag and pin in place around the top edge.

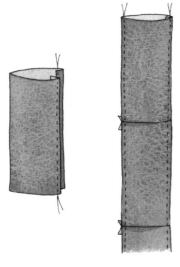

6 The handles are made up using the leftover leg parts of the jeans. Cut strips of 2in (5cm) wide fabric from the length of the jeans and join the strips to make a strap of the length you require. Press ⅜in (1cm) hems on both sides of the strap, fold, and stitch both edges to create long, neat handle strips.

7 Pin the handles in place on each side of the bag, between the lining and the jeans, and sew a neat seam all around the top edge, attaching lining and handles in one go.

CHAPTER 2

constructed block printing

This chapter looks at constructing printing blocks from household and craft materials, from potatoes to children's foam stickers. By carving away some parts of the block and gluing other parts to it, a design is built up on the printing block.

toiletry bag

This is a simple flat-bottomed, zippered bag, but it's made a little taller, so there's plenty of room, and lined with waterproof fabric. The print is a repeated rose, which is a great introduction to layered printing. It's made up of three layers of color: a block color, the outline, and the leaf detail.

---

print ROSES, THREE-LAYER FOAM SHEETS

skill level

1 Prepare your foam sheets as described on page 12. Cut out your main fabric pieces larger than the pattern states and iron them. Apply the print, allowing each layer to dry before you start the next. Once the fabric is completely dry, iron it to set the fabric paint.

2 Cut out the fabric pieces accurately—10in (25cm) along the bottom, 10in (25cm) tall, and then taper both sides until the top measures just 8in (20cm). Make up the handle—fold and press a ⅜in (1cm) hem on both sides of the handle strip, fold in half so that the sides meet, and topstitch (over sew) seams down both sides.

3 Attach your zipper foot to your machine, place the zipper face down along the top edge of one side of the main fabric and sew in place along the edge, right sides facing. Line up the zipper with the top edge of the other side of main fabric and sew in place in the same way.

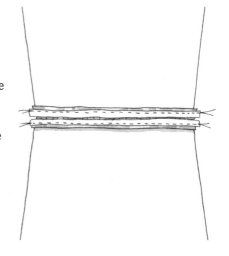

materials

Motifs on page 16

Main fabric

Main panel: cut two, 11in (28cm) square

Handle strip: cut one, 10 x 1½in (25 x 4cm)

Waterproof lining fabric: cut two, 11in (28cm) square

Matching zipper: 8in (20cm)

Matching thread

Craft foam sheets

Three wood or acrylic blocks, 3in (8cm) square

Glue

Sharp knife

Fabric paint

Sponge roller

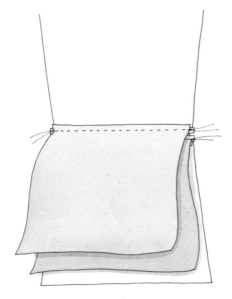

4 To attach the lining to the zipper, repeat the same process, but on the other side of the zipper. Lay your main fabric flat on its wrong side, with the zipper in the center, and press. Place one piece of lining fabric over the top and match its position to the turned over edge of the main fabric, covering the zipper. Pin and sew a neat seam following the same line of stitches as used to secure the main fabric, repeat on the other side. Lay out flat and press.

5 Open out the fabric, matching the lining pieces and the main fabric pieces right sides together. Pin the handle in place between the main fabric pieces, facing inward. With the zipper hidden in the center and the right sides of the fabric pieces together, sew a ⅜in (1cm) seam all around the outer edges leaving a 2in (5cm) gap at the base of the lining and capturing the handle in the seam.

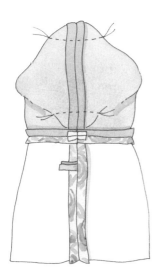

6 On the lining fabric piece, fold the fabric so that the bottom of the bag is flattened, the seam is in the center, and two protruding corner triangles are created. Press flat and sew a diagonal closing seam 1½in (4cm) in from each corner. Repeat this on the main fabric, trim the corners off.

7 Pull the bag through the opening in the lining fabric, turn it right side out, and press the top edge away from the zipper. Sew the opening in the lining closed.

tapered purse

This is a sharply shaped bag with a sharp chevron print! This useful bag has a strong, structured shape and internal pockets to keep all your bits organized.

print CHEVRONS, FOAM SHEET

skill level

materials

Template on page 123

Main fabric

Main panel: cut two, 12 x 10in (30 x 25cm)

Sides: cut two, 3 x 10in (8 x 25cm)

Bottom: cut one, 12 x 3in (30 x 8cm)

Handle strip: cut two, 31½ x 2½in (80 x 6cm)

Lining fabric

Main panel: cut two, 12 x 10in (30 x 25cm)

Sides: cut two, 3 x 10in (8 x 25cm)

Bottom: cut one, 12 x 3in (30 x 8cm)

Pocket pieces: cut two, 12 x 7in (30 x 18cm)

Iron-on interfacing

Cut the same pieces as for the main fabric

Matching thread

Large button

Two foam sheets

Strong board or wooden block

Glue

Scissors or a knife

Fabric paint

1 Prepare your printing block with a chevron pattern using foam shapes as described on page 12. Next, prepare the paper pattern pieces using the templates on page 123. Cut out your main fabric pieces larger than the pattern states and mark your print pattern directly onto the fabric in pencil or dressmakers' chalk. Now print your fabric. When the design is dry, iron the fabric to set the paint. Cut out all of the pattern pieces to size accurately.

2 To stiffen the main fabric, iron on the interfacing following the manufacturer's guidelines.

3 Working with the handle fabric strips, and with the right sides together, sew a ⅜in (1cm) seam on the long sides and one end to close. Trim the corners, then turn right side out. Press and topstitch (over sew) around all sides for a neat finish.

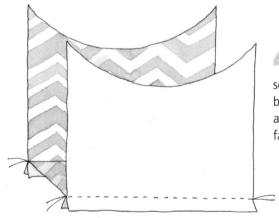

4 Working with the main fabric and with right sides together, sew the base panel to the front and back panels leaving ⅜in (1cm) gaps at each end. Now sew on the main fabric side panels in the same way.

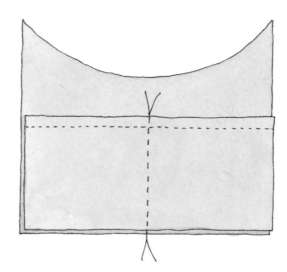

5 Working with the lining fabric, sew the pocket pieces together and press the seams. Topstitch (over sew) the top edge and sew to the right side of the back panel of the lining fabric with a central seam to form the two pockets.

6 Still working with the lining fabric, sew the base panel to the front and back pieces, leaving ⅜in (1cm) gaps at each end. Using the same technique as for the main fabric, sew the side lining panels in place.

7 With the main fabric inside out, pin one strap end in place on the inside of the bag. The strap should point down into the pouch.

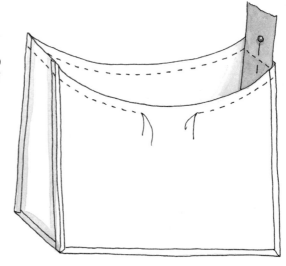

8 Turn the lining right side out and pin it in place around the top inside edge of the main fabric bag. Sew a ⅜in (1cm) seam all around leaving a 4in (10cm) gap in the middle of the back panel to allow for turning.

9 Turn the bag right side out and press the top seam. Topstitch (over sew) the top edge, closing the opening and leaving a neat edge. Machine-sew the loose end of the strap in place on the opposite side of the bag on the outside and attach a button for decoration.

tablet case with handles

This practical, padded carry-case is designed to keep your iPad or tablet protected while you travel; with extra pockets added to store papers and cables. The print design is based on the natural shape of the potato. You could choose a simple rounded shape or a more unusual shape.

Print POTATO PRINT SHAPES

skill level

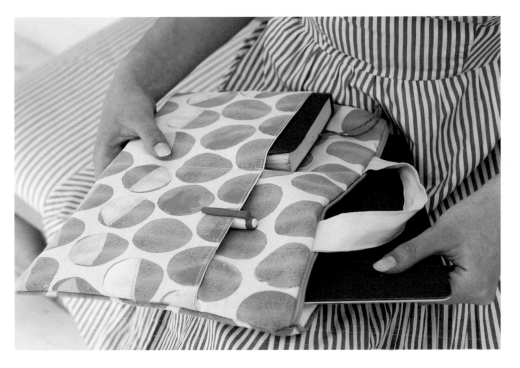

materials

Main panel: cut two, 12 x 10in (31 x 25cm)

Pocket: cut one, 12 x 8in (31 x 20cm)

Handle strips: cut two, 9 x 3in (24 x 8cm)

Lining fabric main panel: cut two, 12 x 10in (31 x 25cm)

Pocket: cut one, 12 x 10in (31 x 25cm)

Batting (wadding): cut two, 12 x 10in (31 x 25cm)

Matching zipper, 12in (30cm)

Matching thread

Potatoes, a selection in a few different sizes

Sharp knife

Paintbrush

Fabric paint

1 Prepare your potatoes as described on page 10. Cut out the main fabric slightly larger than the pattern to allow you to print a larger area. Carefully print the fabric and, once it is dry, iron it to set the fabric paint. You can now cut your pattern pieces to size.

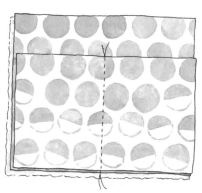

2 Sew the pocket pieces together with a ⅜in (1cm) seam along the top edge, press, and topstitch (over sew) the top edge. Baste (tack) the batting (wadding) into place on both main fabric pieces. Attach the pocket piece to the outside of one of the main fabric pieces by sewing a pocket dividing seam at about 7in (18cm) to one side.

3 Make up the handle straps by pressing a ¼in (6mm) seam allowance along the fabric edges, fold in half, and press together to make long strips. Topstitch (over sew) both sides.

4 Pin the handle strips in place 4in (10cm) in from the edges on the main fabric pieces, facing down. On the right side of the main fabric, pin and sew the zipper in place. Capture the handle straps in the same seam.

5 Sew the lining fabric to the zipper along the same line of stitching. Open the fabric out and match up the lining fabric and main fabric, with right sides together. Sew seams with ⅜in (1cm) seam allowance all around the edges of both the main and the lining fabrics. Make sure you catch the batting (wadding) fabric in this seam. Leave a small opening in the middle of one side seam on the lining for turning.

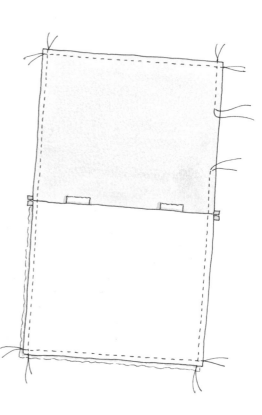

6 Trim all of the corners and turn the bag right side out. Press the whole bag.

puffball purse

This bag has a lovely, soft outline and is a great size for your daily necessities. The print is made using pre-cut foam shapes, easily available in your local craft store. Placing the shapes in a regular sequence creates a leaf pattern, and interest is added by making indents in the foam to make spotty sections.

print LEAF PATTERN, FOAM SHEET   *skill level*

materials

Template on page 122

Main fabric

Top cuff: cut two, 13 x 3in (33 x 8cm)

Bottom piece: cut two, 19 x 9in (48 x 23cm)

Handle strip: 20 x 1½in (51 x 4cm)

Lining fabric

Top cuff: cut two 13 x 3in (33 x 8cm)

Bottom piece: cut two, 19 x 9in (48 x 23cm)

Iron-on interfacing

Top cuff: cut two, 13 x 3in (33 x 8cm)

Matching thread

Pre-cut foam shapes

Wooden or acrylic block, approx. 6in (15cm) square

Glue

Scissors

Fabric paint

1 Prepare your printing block using foam shapes as described on page 12. Then, cut your main fabric to a slightly larger size than the pattern requires so that you can print a slightly larger area and cut it down to size later. Now print your fabric. Make sure that you space the rows evenly; you may need to practice on some scrap fabric first to get it right. Once the fabric paint is dry, iron the fabric to set the paint.

5 Sew a line of stitching with a ¼in (6mm) seam allowance to hold the pleats in place. Repeat this process on all bottom pieces, main fabric and lining fabric.

6 With right sides together, sew the bottom pieces of the main fabric together. Clip the corners.

2 Cut out all of the pattern pieces in the main and lining fabrics, following the pattern template on page 122 for the bottom piece.

3 Following the manufacturer's instructions, iron the interfacing onto the main fabric top cuff pieces to stiffen them slightly.

4 To make the pleats, on all of the bottom fabric pieces, find and mark the center of the fabric, then fold it in on either side of the center by ⅜in (1cm) and pin. Add two more folds on either side, they should be evenly placed and measure ⅜in (1cm) each; keep going until you have reduced your fabric top to measure 13in (33cm), matching the top cuff pattern piece.

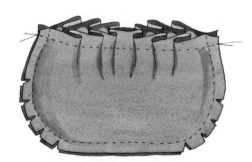

7 With the right sides together, sew ⅜in (1cm) side seams on the top cuff main fabric.

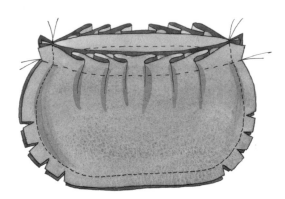

8 Turn the cuff right side out and place it inside the bottom pouch. Pin it to the top edge and sew in place with a ⅜in (1cm) seam allowance. Press the seams. Repeat this process with the lining bottom and cuff pieces.

9 To make the handles, press ⅜in (1cm) seams on both sides of the handle fabric; then fold it in half to match up the edges and topstitch (over sew) down both sides.

10 With the main fabric right sides together and the lining fabric right sides out, place the handle inside the main fabric and pin in place at the sides, insert the lining fabric and pin all around the top edge.

11 Sew a ⅜in (1cm) seam around the top edge (reverse stitch over the handle tabs for extra strength) and leave a small opening—4in (10cm)—in the back seam for turning right side out.

12 Turn the whole bag right side out, press the top seam, and topstitch (over sew) a neat line of stitching to close the opening and finish the bag.

printed panel purse

This simple purse shape is brought to life by the addition of a printed central panel. The print is made up of two basic, hand-drawn ovals that are overlapped and printed in two different shades, creating a complex looking pattern.

print OVERLAPPING OVALS, FOAM SHEET

skill level ○○

1 Prepare your foam sheet printing blocks as described on page 12, using a hand-drawn oval design. Then, cut out the fabric pieces, making the panel that is to be printed slightly larger than needed to make the printing easier. Now print the fabric. Once the print is dry, iron it according to the manufacturer's instructions to set the fabric paint, and then cut the printed panel to the correct size.

2 Following the manufacturer's instructions, iron the interfacing onto the main fabric pieces and the printed panel.

materials

Main fabric:

side panels: Cut two, 15½ x 14½in (40 x 37cm)

Printed panel: cut one, 15½ x 8½in (40 x 22cm)

Lining fabric: cut one, 35½ x15½in (90 x 40cm)

Iron-on interfacing:

side panels: Cut two, 15½ x 14½in (40 x 37cm)

Printed panel: cut one, 15½ x 8½in (40 x 22cm)

Leather for handles—old belts or reclaimed upholstery leather can be used

Matching thread

Foam sheeting

Fabric paint in two colors

Paintbrush

Scalpel or scissors

3 Sew together the side panels and the printed section to make one large rectangle of main fabric. Press the seams and topstitch (over sew) the side panels for a neat finish.

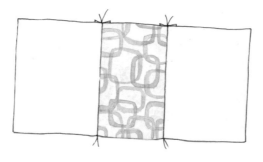

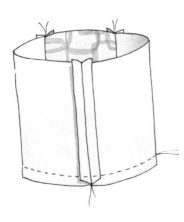

4 Sew up the back seam of the main fabric with a ⅜in (1cm) seam allowance. With the back seam positioned in the center, fold the fabric and press the seam open, then pin and sew the bottom seam closed.

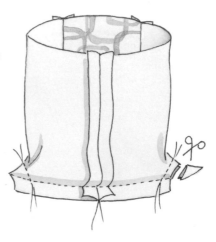

5 With right sides still together, flatten the bag so that the bottom seam runs along the center of the folded section and the corners have protruding triangles. Sew a closing seam 2in (5cm) in from the corner triangle on both sides. Trim off the corners and turn right sides out.

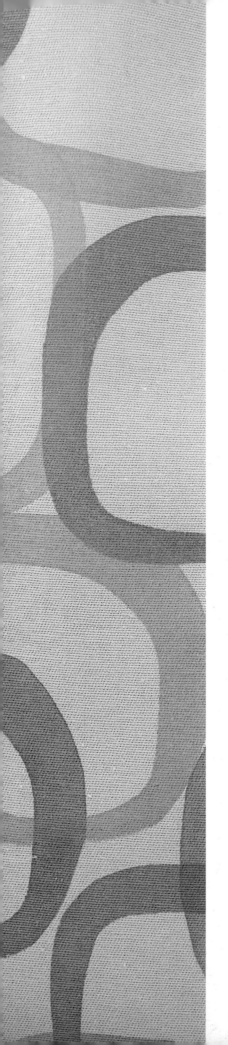

6 With the right sides facing, sew the back seam of the lining fabric. Repeat the same process for assembling the lining bag as you did for the main fabric.

7 Whether you are using leather or fabric strips, you will need to create two handles measuring 20 x 2in (50 x 5cm). (Note that if you are using leather, you need to make sure it's soft enough for your machine to sew through or this design won't work. Alternatively, you could attach the handles after sewing the top seam using studs.) Mark an 8in (20cm) portion of the strap at the center, fold in half, and sew together to form a narrower middle section. Repeat for the other handle.

8 Press the top seam allowance on both the lining fabric and main fabric to create a neat and even top edge.

9 Insert the lining into the main bag and pin together all around the top seam. Insert and pin the handles in place, 4in (10cm) in from the edges on both sides. Neatly sew all around the top edge, finishing the bag and attaching the handles at the same time.

lunch bag

This is a simple idea; a washable bag with waterproof lining ready to carry all your bits for lunch. This is based on the same design as the storage buckets (see page 102) but with a zipper added at the top.

(see page 102)

---

print BOTTLES, POLYSTYRENE TILE

skill level

---

materials

Motifs on page 18

Main fabric: cut one, 26 x 12in (65 x 30cm)

Lining fabric: cut one, 26 x 12in (65 x 30cm)

Iron-on interfacing: cut one, 26 x 12in (65 x 30cm)

Handle strips: approx. 8 x 2in (20 x 5cm)

Main fabric tab ends for zip: cut two, 3 x 4in (8 x 10cm)

Matching thread

Polystyrene tile

Brayer

Fabric paint

1 Prepare your polystyrene tiles for printing as described on page 12. Once you have cut out and pressed your fabric pieces, apply the print. Allow the paint to dry, then iron at a high heat to set.

2 Iron the interfacing onto the main fabric to give it structure. To make the handles, fold and press a ⅜in (1cm) hem down both edges of the handle strips, fold in half, match up the edges, and topstitch (over sew) down both sides to close and finish off. To make the small tabs of fabric to cover the zipper ends, fold a ⅜in (1cm) hem along one edge and press to hold in place. Fold in half with the right sides together and sew a side and top seam with a ⅜in (1cm) seam allowance. Trim the corners and turn right side out. Push the tab over the end of the zipper and sew in place with a square of stitches, repeat for the other tab.

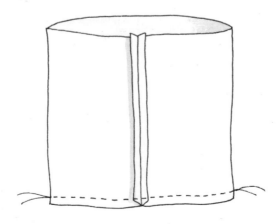

3 Working with the main fabric, fold right sides together and line up the fabric edges. Sew the side edges closed with a ⅜in (1cm) seam. Fold the fabric so that this seam runs down the center back, and press. Sew the bottom seam closed with a ⅜in (1cm) seam.

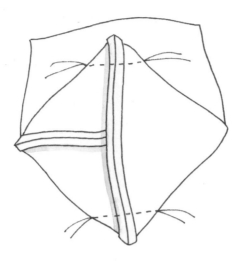

4 Fold the fabric so that the bottom of the bag is flattened, the seam is in the center, and two protruding corner triangles are created. Sew a closing seam 1½in (4cm) diagonally in from each corner. Trim off the corners and turn the bag right side out.

5 Make up the lining in the same way as you did the main fabric bag, but leave the lining inside out when it's assembled and insert it into the main bag pouch.

6 Pin the lining in place all around the top of the bag, then pin the handles in place on either side of the bag. Next, pin the zipper in place on the inside lip of the bag. Using the zipper foot on your sewing machine, sew a neat line of stitches down each side of the zipper attaching all four layers in one!

two-tone shopper

This stylish and practical bag is made using French seams, which are strong and give a great finish. The bag is lightweight, so it will fold away neatly to be stowed in your purse. The print used here is a simple circle; match the fabric paint to the color of the base of the bag for a bold design.

print SPOTS, FOAM SHAPES

skill level

1 Prepare your foam-shape printing blocks as described on page 12. The circle motif used here has a 1in (2cm) diameter. Cut the pattern pieces out of your two fabrics. Set aside the fabric to be used for the base of the bag and print the top fabric pieces. Once the prints are dry, iron the fabric to set the fabric paint.

2 With right sides together, pin the top printed panel pieces and the bottom panel together along the longer edges. The printed panel should overlap the base panel by an extra ⅜ in (1cm). Sew with ¼in (6mm) seams.

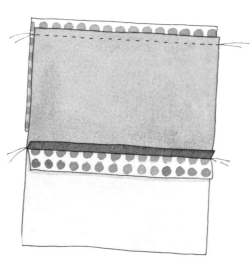

materials

Main fabric base color: cut one, 19½ x 13½in (50 x 35cm)

Main fabric top color: cut two, 19½ x 11¾in (50 x 30cm)

Handle strips: cut two, 23½ x 4¾in (60 x 12cm)

Matching thread

Foam shapes

Wooden or acrylic block

Scissors

Glue

3 Press the seams. On the side of the fabric with raw edge seams, fold the overlap under itself encasing all the raw edges, press, and sew in place.

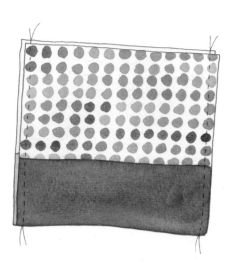

4 Now create the French seams and the box bottom of the bag. First, with the wrong sides together, sew ⅜in (1cm) seams on the sides and bottom of the bag.

5 On the bottom fabric piece, turn and fold the fabric so that the bottom of the bag is flattened, the seam is in the center, and two protruding corner triangles are created. Sew a closing seam 2in (5cm) in from each corner and trim.

6 For the corner triangles, trim the seam to ¼in (6mm), turn right sides facing in, press a crisp seam edge, and sew a ⅜in (1cm) seam enclosing all raw edges.

7 Trim the side seams down to ¼in (6mm), turn right sides in, and press a crisp seam edge. Sew a ⅜in (1cm) seam down the sides enclosing all of the raw edges, turn, and press right side out.

8 To make the handles and finish the top hem, fold the handle strips and sew a ⅜in (1cm) seam along their lengths. Turn right side out, press, and topstitch (over sew) both sides. Mark an 8in (20cm) portion of the strap at the center of its length, fold it in half (just the 8in/20cm), and sew together to create a narrower middle section to the handle. Do this for both handles.

9 Fold and press a seam of 2in (5cm) all around the top edge of the bag. With right sides together, pin the handles in place 4in (10cm) in from each edge of the bag, and with the handle loop facing toward the bottom of the bag. Sew in place with a square of stitches on each handle end—this will only be visible from inside the bag once the top seam is turned under.

10 Turn the bag inside out, fold ¾in (2cm) of the top hem over, and pin it in place to the main body of the bag, sew all around the bag top and press all seams. This neatens the top of the bag and hides the handle ends.

slouchy shoulder bag

This tie-top bag has a great look for summer; it has an easy-going style, with a soft and flowing casual shape. It's perfect for everyday use, and big enough for all your useful bits and pieces!

print OVERLAPPING LEAVES, FOAM SHEET

skill level

materials

Motifs on page 18

Template on page 121

Main fabric: cut one on the fold, 7½ x 32in (19 x 82cm)

Lining fabric: cut one on the fold, 7½ x 32in (19 x 82cm)

Matching thread

Foam sheet

Sharp knife

Wooden or acrylic block

Glue

Sponge roller

Fabric paint

1 Prepare your foam sheet printing blocks as described on page 106. Cut the fabric into large rectangles at first to make the printing easier. Press the fabric and apply the print. Allow the print to dry fully, and then iron on a high setting to set the fabric paint.

2 Cut out the fabric to the actual pattern shapes following the template on page 121. Working with one piece of main fabric and one piece of the lining fabric, place them right sides together and sew a ⅜in (1cm) seam all around the edge of the handles, leaving a ⅜in (1cm) gap at each end. Repeat this process with the other two pieces of fabric.

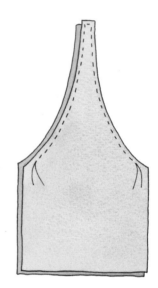

3 Trim the corners and curves, turn the fabric right side out, and press.

4 Leaving the handles right side out, fold out the bag and match the main fabric pieces together and the lining fabric pieces together. Sew around the outside with a ⅜in (1cm) seam leaving a 4in (10cm) opening in the bottom of the lining.

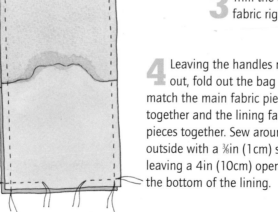

5 Pull the whole bag through the opening, turning right sides out, and sew the opening in the lining closed. To finish, tie the handles at the top.

large shopper

This useful bag folds away when not in use and will hold loads of shopping when needed. You could use any print on this style of bag, but a simple birch tree pattern is used here to complement the gray fabric.

print BIRCH TREES, POLYSTYRENE TILE

skill level

materials

Main fabric

Front and back: cut two, 16½ x 15in (42 x 38cm)

Sides: cut two, 5½ x 15in (14 x 38cm)

Base: cut one, 16½ x 5½in (42 x 14cm)

Front pocket piece: cut one, 9 x 13in (22 x 32cm)

Lining fabric

Front and back: cut two, 16½ x 15in (42 x 38cm)

Sides: cut two, 5½ x 15in (14 x 38cm)

Base: cut one, 16½ x 5½in (42 x 14cm)

Front pocket piece: cut one, 9 x 13in (22 x 32cm)

Iron-on interfacing

Front and back: cut two, 16½ x 15in (42 x 38cm)

Sides: cut two, 5½ x 15in (14 x 38cm)

Base: cut one, 16½ x 5½in (42 x 14cm)

Front pocket piece: cut one, 9 x 13in (22 x 32cm)

Matching thread

Cotton tape: approx. 78in (2m)

Polystyrene tile

Ink roller/brayer

Fabric paint

1 First, cut your pocket piece out of the main fabric and press it ready to print. Prepare your polystyrene tiles for printing as described on page 12, using a hand-drawn birch tree design, and apply the print.

2 Cut out the rest of your pattern pieces and iron the interfacing onto the main fabric base piece. To make up the pocket, take the main fabric piece and the lining piece and, with right sides facing together, sew the top seam, turn, and press. Topstitch (over sew) a neat seam on the top edge.

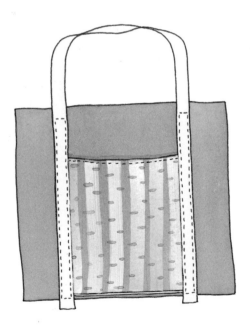

3 Find and mark the center line of the main fabric front piece and lay the newly made pocket piece on its right side. Pin the pocket in place in the bottom center. Pin one length of cotton tape in place around the edge of the pocket—start at the bottom of one side and run the strip up the side of pocket and to the top of the bag, leaving the top 1in (2.5cm) unattached. Run the handle down the other side of pocket and sew it in place along both edges of the cotton tape.

4 Repeat the process from step 3 with the cotton tape on the back panel minus the pocket.

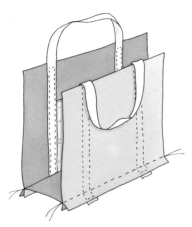

5 With right sides together, sew the base to the front and back panels using ⅜in (1cm) seams and leaving ⅜in (1cm) gaps at each end of the joins. Capture the bottom of the pocket when you're sewing the front piece.

6 Attach the sides to the base by sewing up all four sides with ⅜in (1cm) seams. Turn the bag right side out and press. Fold in a hem of ⅜in (1cm) at the top edge of the bag. Make up the lining for the bag in exactly the same way as you did for the main fabric, without the pocket and tape.

7 Turn the lining right side in and insert it into the main bag. Pin it all around the top edge and sew closed with a neat topstitched (over sewn) seam.

backpack

This classic backpack is very practical and strong. Old belts were used to make the handles, and old key-chain clasps used for the front fixings. The two different fabrics used look great, but you can use one fabric all over if you prefer. Choose a strong fabric, so that you can really get some wear and tear out of this bag.

print TRIANGLES, POTATO PRINT   *skill level*

materials

Main fabric

Top front and back pieces: cut two, 12 x 10in (30 x 25cm)

Bottom front and back pieces: cut two, 12 x 4in (30 x 10cm)

Base piece: cut one, 12 x 6in (30 x 15cm)

Top side piece: cut two, 6 x 10in (15 x 25cm)

Bottom side piece: cut two, 6 x 4in (15 x 10cm)

Side pocket piece: cut two, 8 x 8in (20 x 20cm)

Flap piece: cut one, 12 x 12in (30 x 30cm)

Handle tab: cut one, 3 x 8in (8 x 20cm)

Lining fabric

Top front and back pieces: cut two, 12 x 10in (30 x 25cm)

Bottom front and back pieces: cut two, 12 x 4in (30 x 10cm)

Base piece: cut one, 12 x 6in (30 x 15cm)

Top side piece: cut two, 6 x 10in (15 x 25cm)

Bottom side piece: cut two, 6 x 4in (15 x 10cm)

Side pocket piece: cut two, 8 x 8in (20 x 20cm)

Flap piece: cut one, 12 x 12in (30 x 30cm)

Iron-on interfacing: cut one, 12 x 6in (30 x 15cm)

Matching thread

2 x lengths of cord, 24in (61cm)

10 x large eyelets

Potato

Sharp knife

Fabric paint

TIP Before you start, make sure that your sewing machine can handle sewing through leather. Sew slowly and use a strong needle; try to find thin soft belts. You could also follow the same design with fabric belts.

1 There are many parts to this pattern, so it's best to cut them all out first, and then print on them. Once you have the pattern pieces, lay out the pieces that you are going to print on. Next, prepare a triangle design on your potato stamp as described on page 10 and apply the print. Allow the prints to fully dry before ironing all of the pieces on a high setting to set the fabric paint.

2 Iron the interfacing onto the base main fabric piece. Next, make up all the small elements of the bag. Sew the handle tab by pressing the edges inward by ⅜in (1cm) and top stitching (over sewing) both sides to give a neat finish. Make up the two strips for the front D-ring and key ring fitting. You can use either two strips of leather for this, or fabric tabs measuring 4in (10cm) long and as wide as your D-ring and key ring fittings.

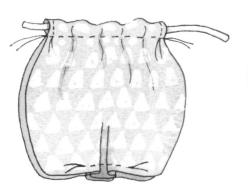

3 Working with the side pockets first, take the main and lining pieces and, with right sides together, sew the top with a ⅜in (1cm) seam. Turn right side out and press—sew another line of stitches, ⅜in (1cm) down from the top edge, creating a channel to house elastic. Thread the elastic through the channel and attach it to one side with a line of stitches. Pull the elastic until the pocket top edge is 6in (15cm) long, pin, and secure to the other side of the pocket with stitches. To finish the pockets, make a central pleat at the bottom of the pocket, making the bottom edge measure 6in (15cm) to match the top edge, sew to secure. Follow this process for the other side pocket.

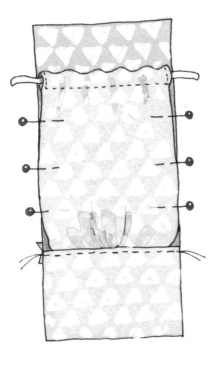

4 Take the top and bottom side panel pieces of the main fabric, place the made-up pocket piece on the right side of the top panel and pin in place to the bottom edge and all along the sides. Place the bottom panel on top of the pocket piece right sides together and sew closed with a ⅜in (1cm) seam, capturing the bottom of the pocket in the same line of stitches. Fold open, press, and topstitch (over sew) the seam for strength. Do this for the other side panel.

5 Next, make up the back piece of the backpack with the buckle ends of the belts. Cut off the buckle ends to 4in (10cm) long. With right sides together, sew the back panel pieces together with the buckles in place—lay the belt wrong side against the main fabric, right side facing upward—with a ⅜in (1cm) seam. Turn and press, and topstitch (over sew) the seam to give extra security to the buckles.

6 The next step is very similar. Working with the front pieces, with right sides together and the D-ring loop in place in the center—facing toward the top edge of the bag— sew together the panels with a ⅜in (1cm) seam. Turn right side out, press, and topstitch (over sew).

7 You can now bring all of these elements together to make up the main bag. Sew the side seams first, with right sides together, and making sure to line up the join in the fabric and to capture the pocket edges within the side seams. Attach the base by sewing, with right sides together, the front bottom edge first and working around the sides and back—leave a ⅜in (1cm) gap at each end to allow you to attach the base to the side pieces.

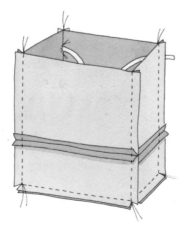

8 Make up all the lining pieces in the same way as you did for the main bag but without the pockets and buckles. Stitch together all the top and bottom parts of the bag, making up four complete panels, and press the seams. While you are sewing up the side seams of the lining, the cord for tying the top of the bag needs to be attached. On the back lining panel piece, 1½in (4cm) from the top, stitch one end of the cord in place facing it in toward the middle of the bag. Do this on both sides— one piece of cord per side. Now sew up the rear side seams, taking care to keep the cords in the center of the bag. Sew up the front side seams and attach the base with ⅜in (1cm) seams all round.

9 Take the main fabric and lining flap pieces and place them with right sides together, and with the key ring fitting at the center front edge pointing inward. Sew a ⅜in (1cm) seam all around the flap, leaving the straight top edge open. Clip the corners and turn right side out. Press and topstitch (over sew) around the edges.

10 You now have all of the elements needed to make up the bag. The "pull-through" method is used to complete it. With the main bag pouch right side facing in, and the lining pouch right side facing out, insert the lining into the main bag. Pin the belt straps in place to the back main fabric, wrong side facing the fabric. Pin the handle tab in place in between the belts ends and pin the flap in place, right sides together, to the back panel of the main bag. Pin the lining all around the main bag top and sew around the top edge with a ⅜in (1cm) seam, leaving an opening on one side for turning. Take care when going over the back because it will be very thick with all the layers of fabric. Reverse stitch over the belts and handles a few times to secure them.

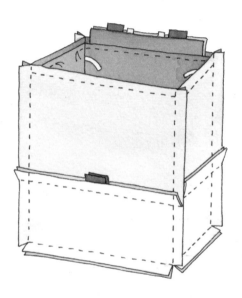

11 Turn the whole bag right side out through the opening and press the top seams, taking care to make sure the flap is held out of the way. Topstitch (over sew) around the top edge to close the opening and give a neat finishing edge.

12 The final step is to make the eyelets for the cord to thread through to close the top. You will need five eyelets on each side. Mark the center front of the bag and place two eyelets an equal distance either side—work toward the back of the bag, placing the remaining four eyelets at regular intervals on each side. Follow the instructions from the eyelet manufacturer and practice on scraps first if you haven't used eyelets before. Thread the cord through the eyelets.

CHAPTER 3

resist printing

Resist printing is a method of printing whereby the ink is blocked from getting to the fabric in certain areas to create the design. In this chapter you will learn about cutting stencils and getting the paint onto the fabric in many different ways, from using a simple sponge to setting up a silk screen.

gathered handbag

In this project, a simple piece of fabric is made to look far more interesting by using pleats. The handle style and pleating mean this bag has an elegant, flowing shape. A classic and simple damask-style repeated pattern is used for this bag.

print DAMASK, STENCIL

skill level

materials

Motif on page 19

Template on page 119

Main fabric: cut two, 17 x 13in (43 x 33cm)

Lining fabric: cut two, 17 x 13in (43 x 33cm)

Bias binding, approx. 5ft (1.5m)

Matching thread

Freezer paper or waxed paper

Low-tack adhesive spray

Sharp knife

Sponge roller

Fabric paint

1 Prepare your stencil as described on page 13. Cut out the fabric pieces slightly larger than your pattern pieces to make the printing easier. Iron your fabric and then print. Once you are happy with your design, allow the fabric to dry completely before ironing to set the paint.

2 Cut out the fabric following the pattern template on page 119. To make the pleats on the lining fabric and main fabrics (four pieces), start by finding the center of the top edge and mark it. Fold in by approximately ⅜in (1cm) on each side of the center and pin. Moving along each side of the top edge, at even increments, fold and pin another four pleats until the whole top edge measures 8in (20cm). Topstitch (over sew) a line of stitches to hold the pleats in place about ¼in (6mm) from the fabric edge.

3 With right sides together, sew a ⅜in (1cm) seam around the curved bottom of the main fabric pieces, leaving a 4in (10cm) opening at either end of the top of the fabric. Repeat this step with the lining pieces and clip the curves on both pouches.

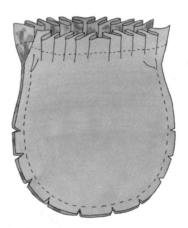

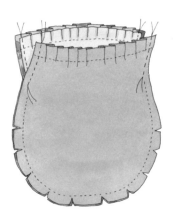

4 Leave the main fabric inside out, but turn the lining fabric right side in. Insert the lining into the main bag pouch, pin, then sew the side openings together with a ⅜in (1cm) seam—leave the gathered top edge open. Turn the bag right side out and press.

5 For the finishing touches, sew the matching bias binding over the gathered edges at the top of the bag—take care to sew through both sides of the binding.

6 To make the handles, take one continuous line of bias binding and secure it in place at one side edge of the bag. Create a 16in (40cm) handle loop, which joins to the other side of the bag, continues straight down the bag edge, and back up the other side to meet the starting point of the bias binding. Make sure that you overlap the ends of the bias binding when it comes around to meet the starting point.

boxy weekender

This bag is all about folding fabric to create an interesting shape. Just one large rectangle of fabric is used to create a roomy box-shaped bag, which is great for an overnight visit, or just when you need a big bag! The print used on this bag is made with a large, layered stencil.

print FOLIAGE, LARGE STENCIL

skill level

1 Prepare your stencils as described on page 13. Cut out your fabric pieces—choose a strong, firm fabric for your main piece because this will hold the shape better and you will not need to interface it. Use the sponge roller to print your fabric, allowing each layer to dry before printing the next. Once your design is dry, iron the fabric to set the fabric paint.

materials

Motifs on page 19

Main fabric: cut one, 40 x 22in (100 x 56cm)

Lining fabric: cut one, 40 x 22in (100 x 56cm)

Iron-on interfacing: 40 x 22in (100 x 56cm) if necessary

Strong cotton tape for the handles, 99 x 1in (2.5m x 2.5cm)

Bias binding, 60in (1.5m)

Matching thread

Matching zipper, 22in (56cm)

Freezer paper or contact paper

Sponge roller

Fabric paint

Scalpel or sharp knife

Dressmakers' chalk

2 Working on the main fabric, mark and pin the handles in place. Find and mark the center of the fabric, measure 5in (12cm) in from the short sides, and mark—this area will be the top of the bag and you do not want to sew handles to this part. Next, pin the handles in place to form a continuous oval approximately 6in (15cm) apart in the center of the bag, leaving the 5in (12cm) areas on either side clear.

3 Sew the handles in place, remembering to reverse stitch over the ends because these will take the most strain. Now sew the zipper in place on the edges of the main fabric (see page 116).

4 Sew the lining fabric onto the zipper, making sure to follow the same line of stitching as for the main fabric, and enclosing the zipper between the main and lining fabrics.

5 Turn right sides out and press. Topstitch (over sew) a line of stitches along the line of the zipper for a neat edge. Take your time, because this edge will be very visible on the finished bag.

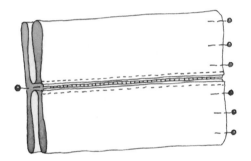

6 Turn inside out again so that the lining fabric is facing out and the main fabric inside. Fold all of the fabric flat with the zipper in the center—measure to make sure you are in the exact center. Mark the center on the bottom piece and mark the inside of the two edges with dressmakers' chalk or a pencil. Fold in the side edges to meet the center mark, creating four layers. Pin in place and repeat on the other side.

7 Sew through all the layers with a ½in (12mm) seam allowance to close. Trim the raw edges and enclose by sewing bias binding or cotton tape over the edges. Turn the whole bag right side out and push out the corners to achieve the boxy shape.

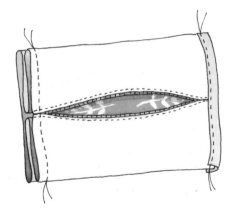

diaper bag

This is just what you need to take the little one out for the day, plenty of room inside for diapers and changes of clothes—there's also a matching changing mat. The print is a rainy day design, but you could choose a pattern to complement your stroller if you wanted to.

print CLOUDS AND RAIN STENCIL AND STAMP

skill level

materials

Main fabric

Front and back panels: cut two, 16 x 11in (41 x 28cm)

Sides: cut two, 4 x 11in (10 x 28cm)

Base: cut one, 16 x 4in (41 x 10cm)

Bellows pockets: cut two, 10 x 8in (25 x 20cm)

Handle strip: cut one, 39 x 4in (1m x 10cm)

Changing mat (optional): cut one, 24 x 14in (60 x 35cm)

Waterproof lining fabric

Front and back panels: cut two, 16 x 11in (41 x 28cm)

Sides: cut two, 4 x 11in (10 x 28cm)

Base: cut one, 16 x 4in (41 x 10cm)

Bellows pockets: cut two, 10 x 8in (25 x 20cm)

Inside pocket pieces cut: cut two, 16 x 8in (41 x 20cm)

Zipper edging: cut two, 14 x 2½in (36 x 6cm)

Iron-on interfacing

Front and back panels: cut two, 16 x 11in (41 x 28cm)

Sides: cut two, 4 x 11in (10 x 28cm)

Base: cut one, 16 x 4in (41 x 10cm)

Bellows pockets: cut two, 10 x 8in (25 x 20cm)

Two magnetic closures

1½in (40mm) D-ring and tribar slide (strap adjuster)

Matching thread

Matching zipper

Toweling, 24 x 14in (60 x 35cm) (optional)

Freezer paper or contact paper

Small eraser

Sharp knife

Lino cutters

Fabric paint

Sponges

1 The main print on this fabric is made with stencil, and an eraser stamp is then used to add raindrops. You will need to draw a basic cloud shape at 2 x 4in (5 x 10cm) and a raindrop that is ¾in (2cm) wide. Prepare your stencil and carved eraser stamp as described on page 13 and 11. Then, cut out your main fabric pattern pieces slightly larger than you need, press, and then print your fabric. Allow the fabric to dry completely before ironing at a high temperature to set the fabric paint.

2 Cut out your fabric to the exact pattern sizes and iron the interfacing onto all of the main fabric pieces.

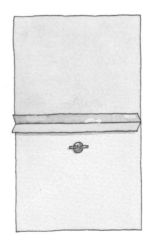

3 The front pockets are bellows pockets with magnetic closings. Working with one piece of main fabric and one lining piece, with right sides together, sew the top seam of the pocket pieces, turn right side out, and press the top edge. Find and mark the center of the top edge of the pockets and, on the lining side, attach the thinner part of the magnetic closing, about ⅜in (1cm) down from the top edge, do this on both pockets.

4 Lay the pockets flat with right sides down, fold both sides in on themselves by 1in (2.5cm) and press. Now fold the folded part back on itself and press again, so you have a concertina effect on each side.

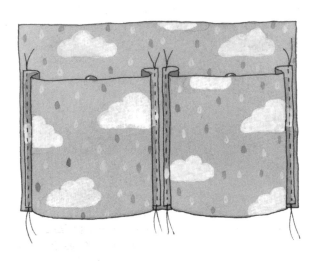

5 Find and mark the center of the front main fabric piece. Place the pockets, lining side down, in the center with their bottom edges aligned. You will need to fold the concertina sides flat to sew the pocket seams to the main fabric. Pin the sides to the main fabric, where they'll naturally lay when the concertina is folded up, and sew in place. The pockets should lay flat when you have finished. Mark the positions of the magnetic closures by pressing the front pockets into the main fabric to leave an indent. Attach the thickest half of the magnetic closure through the main fabric and open out the arms at the back.

6 To attach the base of the bag to the front panel, with right sides together, sew a ⅜in (1cm) seam leaving ⅜in (1cm) gaps at each end. Make sure that you capture the bottom of the pockets in the seam. Reverse stitch over the central seams a few times for extra strength. Sew the back panel and the sides of the main fabric to the base in the same way. Sew the side seams with a ⅜in (1cm) seam, creating the main bag pouch.

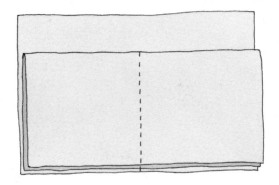

7 To make the internal pockets, fold and press the inside pocket pieces in half and place one each to the lining front and back pieces. Pin them in place and sew the dividing seams where you want them (one seam will give you two pockets, two seams will give you three pockets).

8 To make up the lining, sew the base piece to the front and back pieces with ⅜in (1cm) seams, capturing the pockets pieces and leaving a ⅜in (1cm) gap at each end. Then sew the sidepieces to the base and close all of the side seams.

9 To house the zipper, fold and press a ⅜in (1cm) hem around the zipper-edging piece, fold the whole thing in half, and press. Pin and sew along the edge of the zipper leaving the zipper long at each end. Make small tabs to cover the zipper ends and sew in place with squares of stitches.

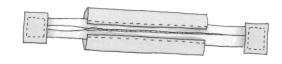

10 Attach the zipper to the lining by sewing it to the right side of the fabric, 1½in (4cm) down from the top edge on either side.

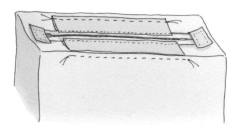

11 To make the handles, fold and press a ⅜in (1cm) hem along both edges of the handle strip and sew a neat edge down both sides. Cut off a 6in (15cm) length to use with the D-ring and leave the rest to attach to the strap adjuster.

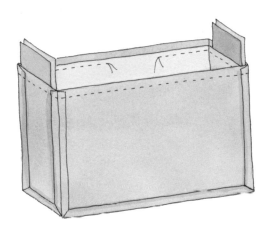

12 The bag is made up using the "pull through" method. The whole bag is made up inside out and then pulled through an opening to finish. With the main bag pouch inside out, turn the lining right side out and insert it into the main bag. Pin it in place all around the top edge of the main bag. At each side, insert the handle tab and strip between the lining fabric and the main fabric. The handles should face down toward the bottom of the bag. Sew a ⅜in (1cm) seam all around the top edge securing the handles and the lining at the same time. Leave a 4in (10cm) opening on the back edge to allow for turning.

13 Pull the whole bag through the opening, press the top edge, and sew a neat seam all around the top to close the opening.

14 If you want to make the matching changing mat, print the main fabric to match the bag and, with right sides together, sew the main fabric and the toweling together all around the outer edge, leaving just a small opening. Trim the corners and pull through the opening. Press the edges and sew a neat edge seam to close the opening and finish.

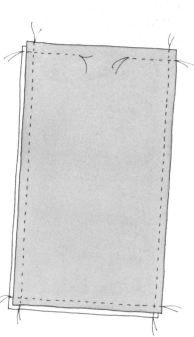

shaped tote bag

This is a great carry-all purse with an attractive rounded shape. Use a strong fabric to give the bag structure. A stencil and masking tape were used to print the design onto this bag—a great way to brighten up a plain fabric.

print SUCCULENTS, STENCIL AND MASKED STRIPS

skill level

materials

Motifs on page 18

Template on page 121

Main fabric: cut two on the fold, 9 x 17in (23 x 43cm)

Lining fabric: cut two on the fold, 9 x 17in (23 x 43cm)

Iron-on interfacing: cut two on the fold, 9 x 17in (23 x 43cm)

Matching thread

Masking tape

Freezer paper

Sharp knife

Sponge roller

Fabric paint

1 Cut your fabric into a rectangle slightly larger than the pattern pieces, use masking tape to define the edges of the stripes, and roll fabric paint straight on. Prepare your stencil for printing as described on page 13 and apply the print. Once the fabric is dry, iron it on a high heat to set the fabric paint. Now cut out the pattern pieces to the exact sizes needed and iron interfacing onto the main fabric if needed.

2 On the pattern pieces, pin pleats in the center of the fabric beneath the handle. Secure the pleats with a line of stitches ¼in (6mm) from the top edge.

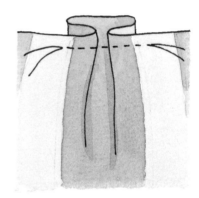

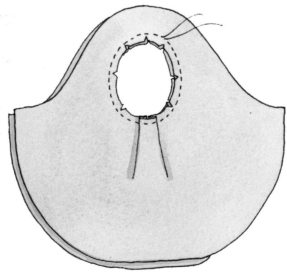

3 Working with one piece of main fabric and one piece of lining fabric, and with the right sides together, pin and sew a ⅜in (1cm) seam around the inside edge of the handle hole. Clip the curved edges, pull the lining out through the hole, and smooth out. Press, and topstitch (over sew) the inside edge to secure and neatly finish the edge. Do this for both sides of the bag.

4 Match up the main fabric pieces and lining fabric pieces—opening the bag out into a sort of figure-eight shape. With right sides together, sew a ⅜in (1cm) seam around the outer edges of both the main and lining fabrics, leaving a gap in the stitching to turn out. Clip the curves.

5 Turn the whole bag right side out and press. Press a ⅜in (1cm) fold around the whole top edge of both the main and lining fabrics so that they meet neatly, pin, and sew closed all around the top edge of the handle. If you prefer, you could use bias binding here.

roll storage

This is a neat little idea for storing loose picnic cutlery, but you could apply the same idea to storage bags for knitting needles, paintbrushes, or craft tools. You can adjust the size for whatever you require.

print CUTLERY, STENCIL

skill level

materials

Motifs on page 16

Main fabric: cut one, 16½ x 10½in (42 x 27cm)

Lining fabric

Main panel: cut one, 16½ x 10½in (42 x 27cm)

Pocket piece: cut one, 16½ x 6in (42 x 15cm)

Cotton tape for handles, approx. 30in (76cm)

Matching thread

Freezer paper or parchment paper and low-tack spray

Fabric paint

Sponges

Sharp knife

1 Prepare your stencil as described on page 13. Prepare your fabric by cutting it to size and ironing it. Apply your print design, and once the paint has dried fully, iron the fabric on a high heat to set the paint.

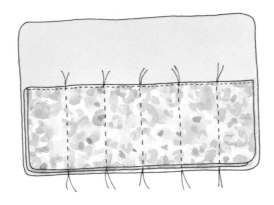

2 Fold your pocket piece in half, press, and topstitch (over sew) the top edge. Place the pocket piece on top of the main lining piece, pin it to hold it in place, and sew dividing lines where you need them for your specific requirements.

3 Cut the cotton tape into three pieces: two 12in (30cm), and one 6in (15cm) long for the handle. On the main fabric, attach the tie strip facing toward the right-hand side of the fabric, 10in (26cm) in from the right edge and 5in (13cm) up from the bottom edge. Sew it in place with a square of stitches. Pin the handle and the other tie strip in place to the left-hand side of the main fabric. Pin the tie in the center and evenly place the handle's ends to either side.

4 With right sides together, sew the main fabric to the lining fabric with a ⅜in (1cm) seam, making sure to catch the handle and the dividing pocket piece in all of the seams. Leave a 4in (10cm) gap in the stitching at the end of the fabric without the handles.

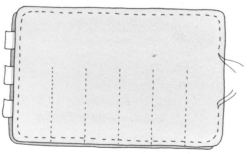

5 Trim the corners, turn right side out, and poke out the corners so that they're correctly shaped. Flatten and press the bag. Topstitch (over sew) around the edges to close the opening and finish with a neat edge.

wine gift bag

A reusable wine bottle bag is a great gift. You could make it seasonal or personalize it by choosing a different print design, A large, funky flower design was used for this one, perfect for a spring or summer gift. Choose a strong fabric, such as canvas, denim, or burlap.

print LARGE FLOWER, STENCIL AND ERASER STAMP

skill level

1 The main print on this fabric is made with stencil, and an eraser stamp is then used to add details. Prepare your stencil and carved eraser stamp as described on pages 13 and 11. Cut out the main fabric slightly larger than the pattern (you'll cut out the handle detail after printing), press your fabric, and apply the print. Once the fabric paint is dry, iron the fabric on a high heat to set the paint.

2 Now cut out the main pattern pieces accurately. For the handle shape, use the template on page 120.

3 Take one main fabric piece and one lining piece and, with right sides together, sew a ⅜in (1cm) seam around the inside line of the handle holes. Clip the corners and turn right side out by pulling the lining through the hole. Smooth the fabric in place and press the edges. Topstitch (over sew) around the inside edge of the hole to secure and leave a neat finish.

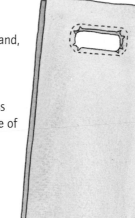

materials

Motifs on page 17

Template on page 120

Main fabric: cut two, 7½ x 18in (19 x 46cm)

Lining fabric: cut two, 7½ x 18in (19 x 46cm)

Matching thread

Freezer paper or contact paper

Sharp knife

Large eraser or sheet of rubber block

Lino cutters

Fabric paint

Sponges

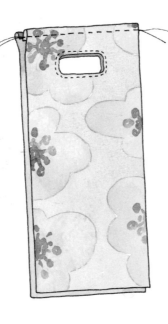

4 Fold the top edges of the main and lining fabrics over by ⅜in (1cm), press, and sew together to finish off the top edge. Repeat steps 3 and 4 to make the other piece.

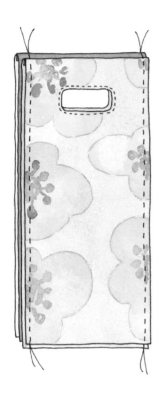

5 French seams are used to make up the bag. Take your two pieces of fabric, place them wrong sides together, and sew a ⅜in (1cm) seam down both sides. Trim the seam edges so that they are as narrow as you can make them without compromising the stitches. Turn inside out and press the seams. Sew another ⅜in (1cm) seam down the sides enclosing all the raw edges inside.

6 Leaving the bag inside out, sew a ⅜in (1cm) seam across the bottom edge to close. Fold the fabric so that the bottom of the bag is flattened, the seam is in the center, and two protruding corner triangles are created. Sew a closing seam ¾in (2cm) diagonally in from each corner. Trim off the corners and turn the bag right side out.

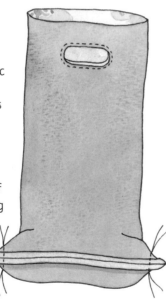

men's messenger bag

Roomy inside with a large flap to cover all of your belongings, this bag is a simple shape, based on the classic messenger bag. A kooky repeat pattern of mustaches is printed in black on natural linen fabric.

print MUSTACHES, STENCIL SCREEN PRINT

skill level

materials

Motifs on page 19

Main fabric

Main body: cut one, 26 x 14in (66 x 36cm)

Front panel: cut one, 14 x 14in (36 x 36cm)

Front pocket: cut one, 16 x 15in (41 x 38cm)

Flap: cut one, 14 x 14in (36 x 36cm)

Lining fabric

Main body: cut one, 26 x 14in (66 x 36cm)

Front panel: cut one, 14 x 14in (36 x 36cm)

Front pocket: cut one, 16 x 15in (41 x 38cm)

Flap: cut one, 14 x 14in (36 x 36cm)

1½in (40mm) D-ring

1½in (40mm) tribar slide (strap adjuster)

1½in (40mm) cotton tape, approx. 39in (1m)

Freezer paper or contact paper

Small silk screen

Squeegee

Fabric paint

1 Cut out all of the fabric pattern pieces and press the flap and front pocket pieces ready to print. Prepare your stencils and screen as described on page 13. If you don't have access to a screen, you could sponge the fabric paint on. Once the print is dry, iron it at a high heat to set the fabric paint.

2 To construct the front pocket piece, take the main and lining fabric pattern pieces and, with the right sides together, sew the top edge with a ⅜in (1cm) seam. Turn, press, and topstitch (over sew) for a neat edge. Place the made-up pocket on the top of the front bag panel, pin in place, and sew a central dividing seam. Sew what will be the bottom of the pocket by working a line of stitches 2½in (6cm) up from the bottom edge.

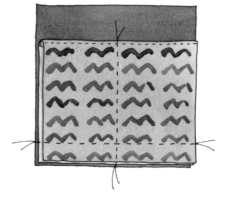

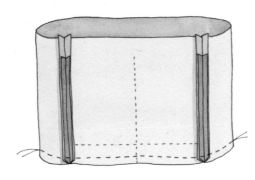

3 To make up the main bag, with right sides together, sew two ⅜in (1cm) seams, attaching the front panel to the main body of the bag, capturing the pocket pieces in the seams. Fold the bag so that the front panel is central and sew the bottom edge closed with a ⅜in (1cm) seam.

4 To flatten the bottom of the bag, fold the fabric so that the bottom of the bag is flattened, the seam is in the center, and two protruding corner triangles are created. Press the fold and sew a closing seam 2in (5cm) in from each corner and trim off the corners.

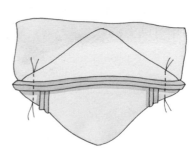

5 Make up the lining pieces in the same way, sewing the front panel to the main body pieces, closing the bottom seam, and then using the triangle corners to make the flat bottom of the bag.

6 Cotton tape is used for the handles but you could make your own from matching fabric—the strap needs to be 39in (1m) in length and 1½in (4cm) wide. Cut a 4in (10cm) length of the cotton tape and thread it through the D-ring. Sew the ends to secure.

7 To make the top flap, with the right sides of the flap pieces facing together, sew a ⅜in (1cm) seam around the two sides and bottom edge. Trim the corners and turn right sides out, press, and topstitch (over sew) a line of neat stitches to finish, leave the top edges raw as they will be hidden inside the bag.

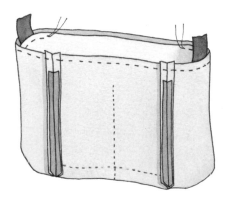

8 The bag is made up using the "pull-through" method. With the main fabric still right sides facing in and the lining fabric right sides out, insert the lining into the main bag pouch. Pin the handle tab with the D-ring to one side of the bag facing down, and pin the handle strip of cotton tape to the other side of the bag, also facing down. Pin the lining in place around the top edge of the bag. Sew a ⅜in (1cm) seam all around the top edge of the bag leaving a 15in (38cm) opening centrally at the back to allow turning, and for attaching the flap. Turn the bag right side out and press the top edge.]

9 Insert the flap into the opening and pin it in place. Now sew all around the top edge with a neat seam to attach the flap, close the opening, and finish off the bag. Thread your strap through the tribar, pass it through the D-ring, and attach the loose end to the central bar of the tribar slide.

rounded shoulder bag

This is a very practical and cute little shoulder bag—it's perfect for throwing your essentials into and slinging over you shoulder when you're on the go. The print used on this is the ever-popular bird on a branch, a simple silhouette with added color spots for berries.

print BIRD ON A BRANCH, STENCIL   *skill level*

materials
Motif on page 17

Templates on page 125

Main fabric

Front and back: cut two, 11 x 9in (28 x 23cm)

Outer pocket: cut one, 11 x 7in (28 x 18cm)

Flap: cut one, 10 x 9in (25 x 23cm)

Lining fabric

Front and back: cut two, 11 x 9in (28 x 23cm)

Outer pocket: cut one, 11 x 7in (28 x 18cm)

Flap: cut one, 10 x 9in (25 x 23cm)

Iron-on interfacing

Front and back: cut two, 11 x 9in (28 x 23cm)

Outer pocket: cut one, 11 x 7in (28 x 18cm)

Flap: cut one, 10 x 9in (25cmx23cm)

Strap fabric (see step 6)

Matching thread

Freezer paper

Sharp knife

Pencil with eraser

Fabric paint

Sponge

1 Prepare your stencils as described on page 13. Apply the stencils and print the berries using the eraser on the end of a pencil as a stamp. Once the whole design is dry, iron on a high heat to set the fabric paint.

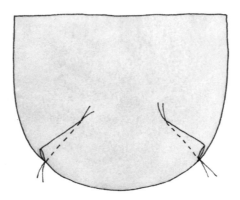

2 Cut out the rest of your fabric pieces and iron the interfacing onto the main fabric pattern pieces. Sew the darts closed on all of the main and lining fabric pieces—to do so, fold the fabric right sides together, line up edges and sew a ⅜in (1cm) seam to close the darts.

3 With right sides together, sew the outer pocket pieces (main fabric and lining) together along the top edge with a ⅜in (1cm) seam. Turn right side out, press the seam, and topstitch (over sew) along the top edge for a neat finish. Pin the made up pocket piece to the main front fabric piece, making sure to line up the darts, and then sew it in place with a central seam, creating two pockets.

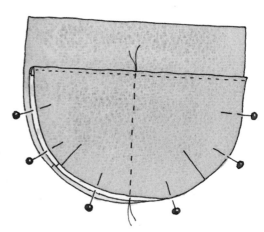

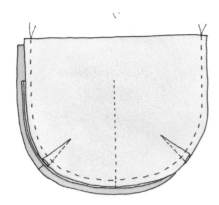

4 Take the front and back main fabric pieces for the body of the bag and, with right sides together, pin and sew a ⅜in (1cm) seam around the outer edge. Take care to line up the dart seams and to capture the pocket edges within the seam.

5 To make up the flap, with right sides together, sew the printed main fabric to the lining with a ⅜in (1cm) seam around the outer edge. Leave the straight top edge open. Clip the corners, turn right side out, and press. Topstitch (over sew) the edges of the flap to finish. Now sew the main pouch lining pieces together in the same way as you did the main bag. Trim all of the curved edges.

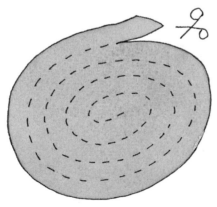

6 To make up the strap, you first need to decide how you would like it to look— for fabric handles, make up a long main fabric strip, 2in (5cm) wide. To do this, first cut a strip 3½in (9cm) wide, press, and fold and sew the edges to create a neat strip. If you are going to use leather braids like the ones shown here, cut a long strip of leather. If you don't have leather strips you can make long strips by cutting a spiral from a smaller scrap. Try to cut as evenly as possible, but with some rough edges—it looks good for this strap.

7 To braid the leather, with three strips, machine sew one end about 2½in (6cm) in (if your machine is strong enough to do so, if not, tie the ends), and then tightly braid the strips to the length of strap you want. To secure, sew or tie closed leaving 2½in (6cm) free at the end.

8 You will need to make small tabs to poke out of the bag to which you can tie the straps. Use leather or fabric to do this—cut a strip of your chosen material as wide as the D-rings you are going to use and 6in (15cm) long. Thread the strip through the D-ring and sew at the base to secure. Make two tabs in total, one for each end of the strap. The tabs are attached when the top seam of the bag is sewn.

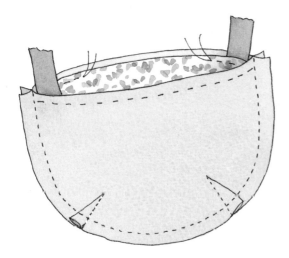

9 You can now finish making up the bag. This is done using the "pull-through" method. With the main pouch still right side facing in, tuck the handle tab ends into the sides, pointing down into the bag and pin them in place. With the lining pouch turned right side facing out, insert it into the main bag and pin it in place around the top edge of the bag. Sew a ⅜in (1cm) seam around the front and sides of the bag, securing the handle tabs in place. Leave an opening of 10in (25cm) along the back edge for turning and attaching the flap.

10 Turn the whole bag right side out and press the top edge. Insert the flap into the 10in (25cm) opening, pin, and sew a neat seam all around the top edge of the bag, securing the flap, closing the opening, and neatly finishing the top edge. To finish, tie or stitch the strap to the D-rings depending on the style of strap you have chosen.

bucket storage bags

This set of bucket bags is a great storage solution for any room. The soft buckets stand up by themselves and have handles so that you can carry them around. There are three sizes here; you can make them all or choose the size most useful to you.

materials

Motifs on page 17

Main fabric

Large bucket: cut one, 33½ x 16in (85 x 40cm)

Medium bucket: cut one, 26 x 12in (65 x 30cm)

Small bucket: cut one, 18 x 10in (45 x 25cm)

Lining fabric

Large bucket: cut one, 33½ x 16in (85 x 40cm)

Medium bucket: cut one, 26 x 12in (65 x 30cm)

Small bucket: cut one, 18 x 10in (45 x 25cm)

Medium-weight iron-on interfacing

Large bucket: cut one, 33½ x 16in (85 x 40cm)

Medium bucket: cut one, 26 x 12in (65 x 30cm)

Small bucket: cut one, 18 x 10in (45 x 25cm)

Leather strips or cotton tape for handles, approx. 12 x 1½in (30 x 4cm) per handle

Matching thread

Freezer paper

Screen

Squeegee

Fabric paint

1 These bags are printed using a stencil and a screen to give a professional finish. Prepare your stencils and screen as described on page 13. If you don't have access to a screen, you could sponge the fabric paint on. Cut out and press your fabric and apply the print. Once the fabric is dry, iron it at a high heat to set fabric paint.

2 Iron the interfacing onto the main fabric. Now make up the handles: cut your leather into equal strips, two for each bucket. If you are using cotton tape, cut it to length. Alternatively, you could make the handles from matching fabric by cutting a strip 2 x 8in (5 x 20cm), folding and pressing a ⅜in (1cm) hem on each side, and folding over and sewing down both edges to finish.

3 Working with the main fabric, fold right sides together and line up the fabric edges. Sew the side edges closed with a ⅜in (1cm) seam. Fold the fabric out so that this seam runs down the center back, and press. Sew the bottom seam closed with a ⅜in (1cm) seam.

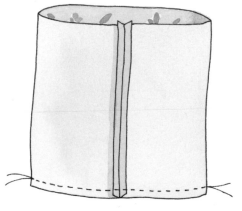

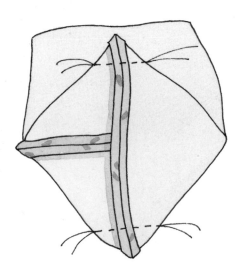

4 Fold the fabric so that the bottom of the bag is flattened, the seam is in the center, and two protruding corner triangles are created. Sew a closing seam diagonally in from each corner: 3in (7.5cm) for large; 2in (5cm) for medium; 1in (2.5cm) for small. Trim off the corners and turn the bag right side out.

5 Make up the lining in the same way as for the main fabric, but leave the lining inside out when made up and insert it into the main bag pouch.

6 Fold over and press a ⅜in (1cm) hem all around the top edge of both the main and lining fabrics. Pin the handles in place inside the main fabric, then pin the lining in place all around the top edge. Sew a neat seam, securing the handles and lining all in one go.

CHAPTER 4

other printing methods

There are many more diverse ways to print onto fabric and in this chapter a further selection of methods is demonstrated. You can try using leaves straight from the garden, your inkjet printer, and even the sun to create fabulous printed fabrics.

simple coin purse

This simple lined purse is a good introduction to working with linings and zippers; once you've mastered them you can attempt many more complicated projects. The print design for this purse is made on the computer, layering images together, then printed out onto photo-transfer paper and ironed onto your fabric.

print VINTAGE POSTCARD, PHOTO TRANSFER   *skill level*

1 Prepare your photo-transfer print as described on page 14. Then, cut out your fabric slightly larger than your transfer image and iron it before you attach the transfer. Iron the transfer image onto the fabric according to the manufacturer's instructions and remove the backing paper. Take care not to apply direct heat to the image throughout the rest of the making process.

2 To attach the zipper, change to the zipper foot on your sewing machine, place the zipper face down along a top edge of the main fabric, and sew in place with a neat seam along the edge. Line up the zipper with the other top edge and sew in place in the same way.

materials

Postcard image on page 126

Main fabric: cut two, 8 x 6in (20 x 15cm)

Lining fabric: cut two, 8 x 6in (20 x 15cm)

Matching zipper, 6in (15cm)

Matching thread

Iron-on photo-transfer paper

Inkjet printer

Iron

Scissors

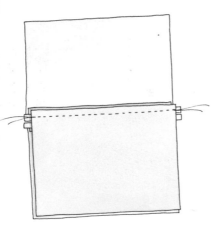

3 To attach the lining, repeat the previous step but on the other side of the zipper. Lay your main fabric flat on its back with the zipper in the center and press flat (be careful with your photo transfer—keep it cool and only apply light pressure). Match one piece of lining fabric to the top edge of the zipper, so it is covering the zipper, pin, and sew a neat seam following the same line of stitches as for the main fabric. Repeat this on the other side with the other piece of lining fabric. Lay the whole purse out flat and press the zipper edges.

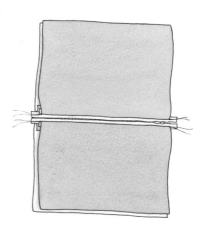

4 Open out the fabric matching the edges of the lining and the main fabric pieces right sides together. With the zipper concealed in the center, sew a ⅜in (1cm) seam all around the outer edges, leaving a 2in (5cm) gap on the bottom edge of the lining for turning.

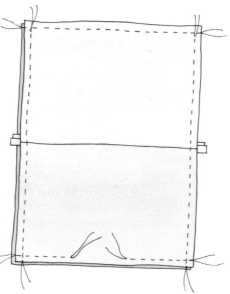

5 Trim the corners and pull the whole purse through the opening in the lining, turning it right side out. Sew the opening in the lining closed, and then push the lining inside the purse.

zippered wallet

This is such a versatile wallet; it could be used to hold coins and cards, or be used as a case for sewing needles and threads. A real fern leaf was used for this print; the paint was rollered directly on the leaf and then the leaf pressed onto the fabric.

skill level

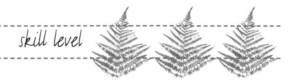

materials

Main fabric: cut one, 8¼ x 7in (21 x 18cm)

Zipper tab ends: cut two, 3½ x 2½in (9 x 6cm)

Lining fabric

Main panel: cut one, 8¼ x 7in (21 x 18cm)

Pocket pieces: cut two, 7 x 6in (18 x 15cm)

Small pocket pieces: cut two, 7 x 5in (18 x 13cm)

Zipper, 18in (45cm)

Bias binding, 3ft (1m)

Iron-on interfacing

Matching thread

Fern leaf for printing

Sponge roller

Fabric paint

Brayer or rolling pin

1 Cut out all of the pattern pieces in the main and lining fabrics, making sure to add curved corners—you can do this by using a compass or drawing around a plate edge, as long as they all match it doesn't matter what size or shape you use. Then, print the fabric with your leaves, following the process described on page 14. Once your design is complete, allow the fabric to dry before ironing it on a high heat to set the fabric paint.

2 Iron the interfacing onto the main fabric to give it more structure. Now, press the pocket fabric pieces in half, layer onto the right side of the lining fabric, pin in place, and sew dividing seams where you want them.

3 Pin the lining fabric to the main fabric wrong sides together, and begin to attach the zipper. Open the zipper fully, then find and mark the center of the purse at both side edges, this is where your zipper will begin and end. Pin the zipper in place around all sides, meeting at the other side and leaving a long end on the zipper to cover later. It's important that the zipper isn't twisted or laying unevenly—test the zipper by closing it while it is just pinned to see if everything lines up correctly. When you are happy, sew the zipper in place all around the outer edge.

4 Sew bias binding all around the purse to house any raw edges. Start near the end of the zipper and make sure to pull it tight around the corners.

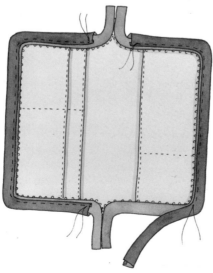

5 Finally, add covers to the zipper ends. Take your strips of main fabric and fold with the right sides together, sew the top and one side of the tab, trim corners, and turn right side out. Fold under the raw ends and press. Slot the cover over the zipper end, pin in place, then sew a square of stitches to secure.

everyday tote bag

This classic tote bag is easy to make and always useful to have around. The sun was used to print this fabric. Amazing designs can be created using a special light-sensitive liquid that just needs to be exposed to the sun.

1 First, cut out your fabric pattern pieces, and then prepare and carry out the cyanotype printing process as described on page 15. The print used here is made using a lace curtain. Once the print is dry, press the fabric.

2 Make up the handles so that they are ready to use at the end. Fold and press ⅜in (1cm) hems on both sides of the handle strips, fold, and press in half matching up the edges. Topstitch (over sew) a neat seam down both sides to finish.

materials

Main panel: cut two, 18 x 16in (45 x 40cm)

Handle strip: cut two, 2 x 8in (5 x 20cm)

Matching thread

Cyanotype chemicals or cyanotype kit

Sponge

Piece of lace curtain

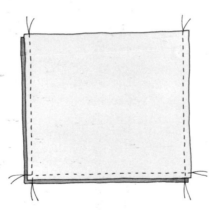

3 Next, make up the main body of the bag. French seams are used so that all raw edges will be hidden. Take your two main pieces of fabric and place them wrong sides together. Sew a ⅜in (1cm) seam around the two sides and base.

4 Trim the seam edge down so that it is as narrow as you can make it without compromising the stitches, turn the whole bag inside out, and press the seams. Sew another ⅜in (1cm) seam around the edges and base enclosing all the raw edges inside. Turn right side out and press again—these are your finished French seams!

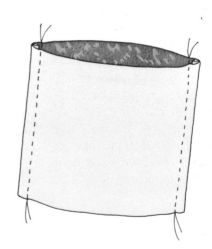

5 Fold the top edge of the bag inward and press a hem of ⅜in (1cm) around the top. Then fold again adding another hem about 1¼in (3cm) enclosing the first hem inside. Take the handles and tuck them into the hem to hide the raw ends. Pin in place and sew all around the base of the hem securing the handles and closing the hem seam. Then sew another line of stitches all around the very top edge to finish.

mini tote bag

This simple little bag is a perfect miniature of Mommy's tote bag, and could have so many uses. Photos of vintage fabric have been turned into iron-on transfers to create this cute bunting design.

print VINTAGE FABRIC BUNTING, PHOTO TRANSFER

skill level ▼ ▼ ▼

materials

Bunting images on page 126

Main fabric

Front and back: cut two, 16 x 18in (40 x 45cm)

Handle strips: cut two, 2½ x 8in (6 x 20cm)

Matching thread

Photo-transfer paper

Inkjet printer

Image program

Iron

1 Cut out the main fabric and press to prepare for printing. Prepare your photo-transfer print as described on page 14. Be careful with your design once you have peeled the backing paper off—do not iron directly onto the transfer.

2 First, make up the handles. Fold and press ⅜in (1cm) hems on both sides of the handle strips, fold, and press in half matching up the edges. Topstitch (over sew) a neat seam down both sides to finish.

3 Make up the main body of the bag—this is done in the same way as for the Everyday tote, see page 110. French seams are used so that all raw edges will be hidden. Take your two main pieces of fabric and place them wrong sides together. Sew a ⅜in (1cm) seam around the two sides and base.

4 Trim the seam edge down so that it is as narrow as you can make it without compromising the stitches. Turn the whole bag inside out and press the seams. Sew another ⅜in (1cm) seam around the edges and base enclosing all the raw edges inside. Turn right side out and press again.

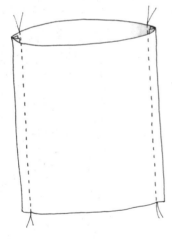

5 Hem the top edge of the bag and attach the handles at the same time. Fold the top edge inward and press a ⅜in (1cm) hem around the top, then fold another hem, about 1¼in (3cm), enclosing the first hem inside. Take your handles and tuck them into the hem to hide the raw ends, pin in place, and sew all around the base of the hem securing the handles and closing the hem seam. Now sew another line of stitches all around the very top of the edge to finish.

sewing techniques

All the equipment used in this book is standard sewing equipment—if you own a sewing machine and have done a little sewing before, chances are that you own everything you need already. If there is a technique or stage you are unsure about, try it out on scrap fabric first so that you don't damage your newly printed fabric by having to unpick several times.

All of the projects in the book are designed to be achievable and enjoyable. If you are a confident sewer, you can adapt the patterns to suit your needs, if you are still learning, then try out a few easy projects first and move up to the harder levels. By the end you will feel ready to tackle anything!

Basic equipment

- Sewing machine with a separate zipper foot attachment
- Sharp scissors
- Seam ripper
- Pins
- Chalk
- Tape measure and ruler
- Iron and ironing board

The sewing techniques

Plain seams—The most basic seam: simply place right sides of the fabric together and sew an even line of stitches along the edge of the fabric. A ⅜in (1cm) seam allowance (the distance between the stitches and the edge of the fabric) is always used in this book unless otherwise stated. Always press your seams open to get a nice smooth finish.

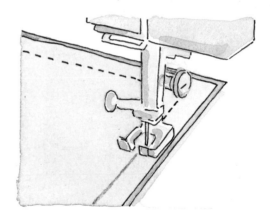

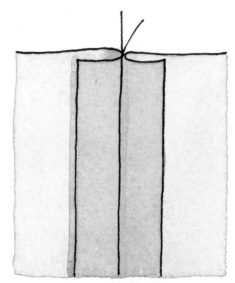

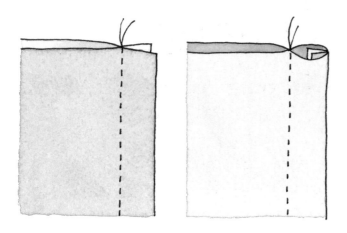

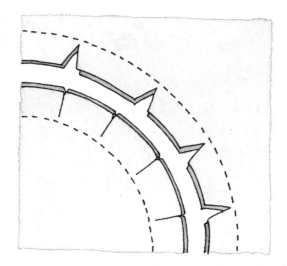

French seams—These look like a plain seam from the outside but all the raw edges are enclosed inside a small, neat channel inside—very good for unlined items. You work in a slightly different way to a plain seam in that you start with the wrong sides of the fabric facing together and sew a plain ⅜in (1cm) seam all along the edge. The seam is then pressed open and the fabric turned out the other way so that right sides are facing together. Then another ⅜in (1cm) seam is sewn enclosing the raw edges within it.

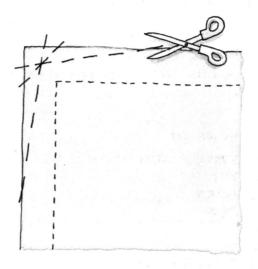

Trimming corners and curves—To help make the fabric lay flat along plain seams, when working around curves you need to clip your seam allowance at regular intervals, taking care not to get too close to the stitches but allowing the fabric to stretch more easily. When working with corners, you must cut away the bulk of the fabric before you turn it right sides out, so that you maintain the sharp corner shape.

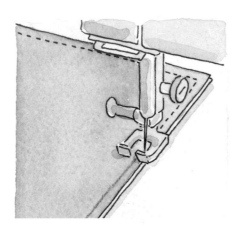

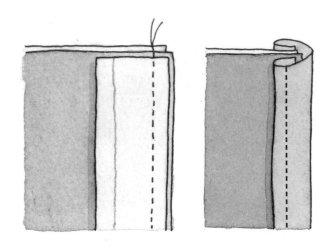

Topstitching or over sewing—This is a decorative stitch but it can also be used to close an opening. Simply sew near to the edge of a closed seam to create a neat finish. It is often used around the top of bags or down the length of handles.

Bias binding edge—This is a neat way to enclose raw edges on the outside of an item. Bias binding strips are available in many colors and widths. Simply pin one raw edge of the binding in place to one edge of the fabric, right sides together, and sew along the fold of the binding to hide stitches. Fold the binding over, enclosing the raw fabric edges of the project, tuck the fold of the binding under, and sew along the other side neatly near the bottom of the binding, to finish.

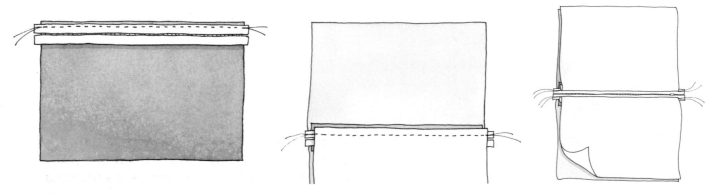

Sewing in a zipper—For the projects in this book, zippers are attached to both the lining and main fabrics before making up the bag structure. To do this, change to your zipper foot on your sewing machine, place the zipper face down along a top edge of the main fabric, and sew in place with a neat seam all down the edge. Next, line up the zipper with the other top edge on the main fabric and sew in place in the same way. To attach the lining to the zipper, repeat the previous steps but on the other side of the zipper. Lay your main fabric flat on its back with the zipper in the center and press flat, match one piece of lining fabric to the top edge of the zipper, lay it so that it is covering the zipper, pin, and sew a neat seam following the same line of stitches as used to secure the main fabric in place. Repeat this on the other side, lay out the whole purse flat and press the zipper edges.

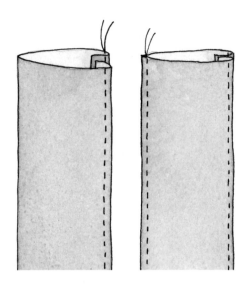

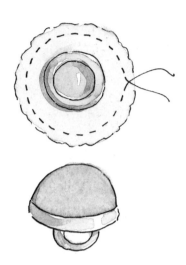

Making fabric handles and straps—Making handles from matching fabric gives a nice seamless finish to a project; this is a simple procedure and it's advisable to make them longer than needed and cut them down later. Cut out your strip according to the size the pattern requires, press a ⅜in (1cm) hem along both sides, fold, and press the whole strip in half matching up the edges. Sew a neat line of topstitch (over sewing) along the open edge, then sew another line of stitches along the closed edge giving a neat, professional finish.

Covering a button—This is a nice finishing touch to a project. Metal and plastic self-cover buttons are readily available in a variety of sizes—just check your local crafts/sewing store. Cut out a circle of your fabric that is ⅜in (1cm) wider than the button and hand sew a running stitch around the outer edge of the fabric. Place the fabric over the button and pull the stitches tight, gathering the fabric around the button. Hold the fabric firmly in place and snap on the back plate.

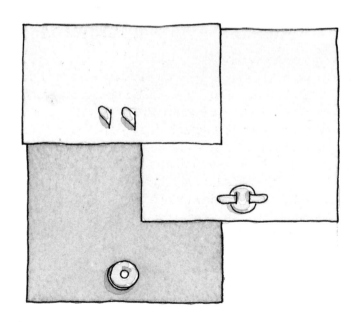

Magnetic closings—These are handy little things to master. They are easy to fit but it's worth buying one extra to practice on with scrap fabric the first time you do it, so that you can see and feel how it works. Mark where you want the closing to go and cut two small slits for the arms, push through the fabric, slide over backing plate, and fold out the arms to secure in place. Repeat the process where you want the other side of the closing to go.

templates

To use the templates on these pages, most of them first need to be enlarged on a photocopier; all the enlargements are detailed next to each template. Cut out the shape from the photocopy, pin this pattern to your fabric, and cut around it. If the template has a line with two arrows, it is only for half the piece. You need to fold the fabric in half on the straight grain, place that edge of the pattern directly on the fold, and then pin and cut through both layers (but don't cut along the fold line.) When you unfold it, you have the complete piece.

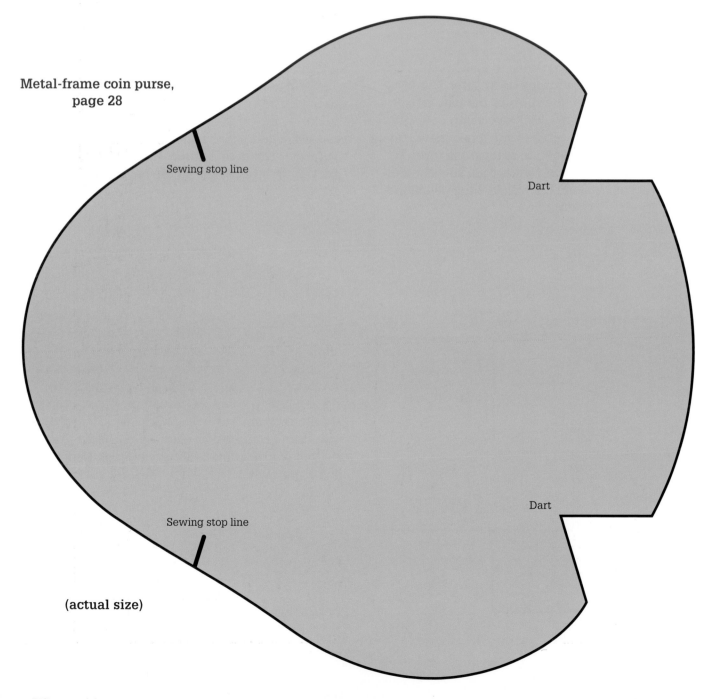

Metal-frame coin purse, page 28

Sewing stop line

Dart

Sewing stop line

Dart

(actual size)

Metal-frame bag, page 14

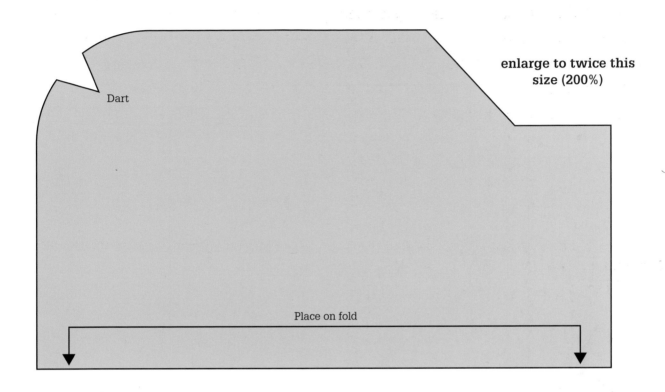

enlarge to twice this
size (200%)

Dart

Place on fold

**Gathered handbag,
page 72**

enlarge to twice this
size (200%)

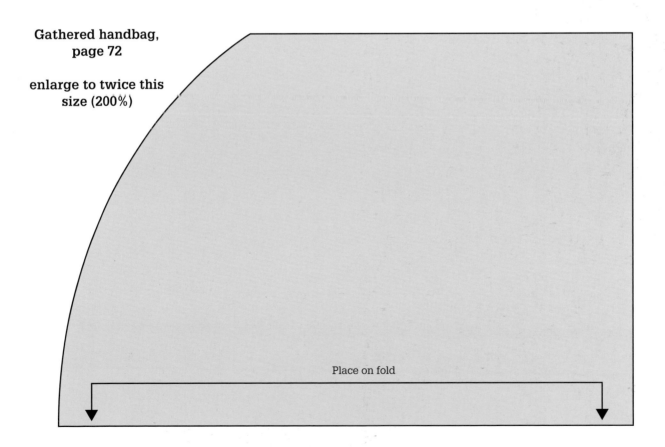

Place on fold

Wine gift bag, page 84

enlarge to twice this
size (200%)

Slouchy shoulder bag,
page 62

Shaped tote bag,
page 80

enlarge to four times
this size (400%)

enlarge to four times
this size (400%)

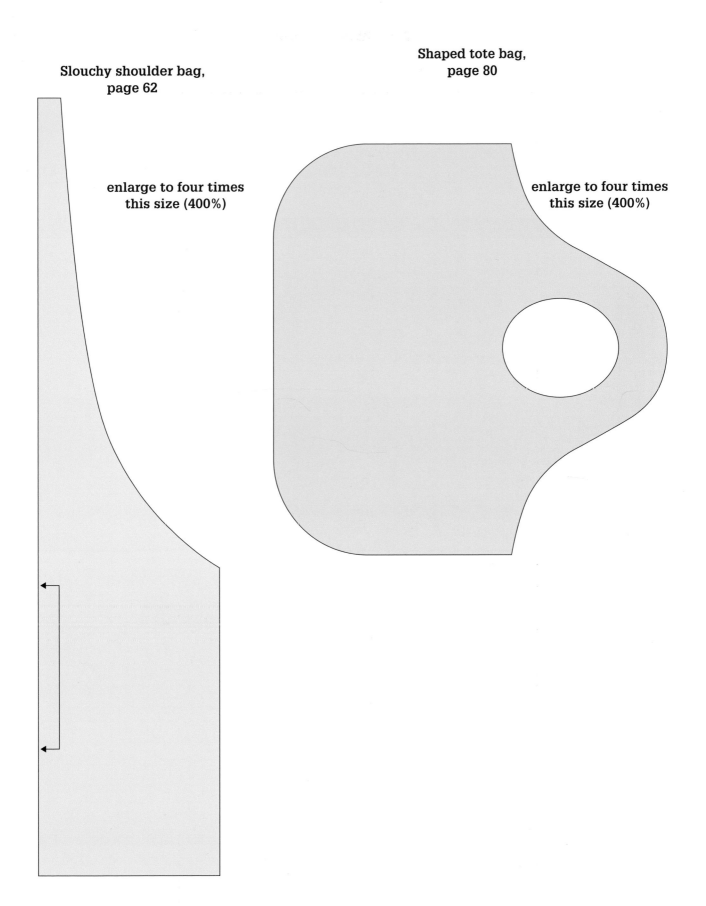

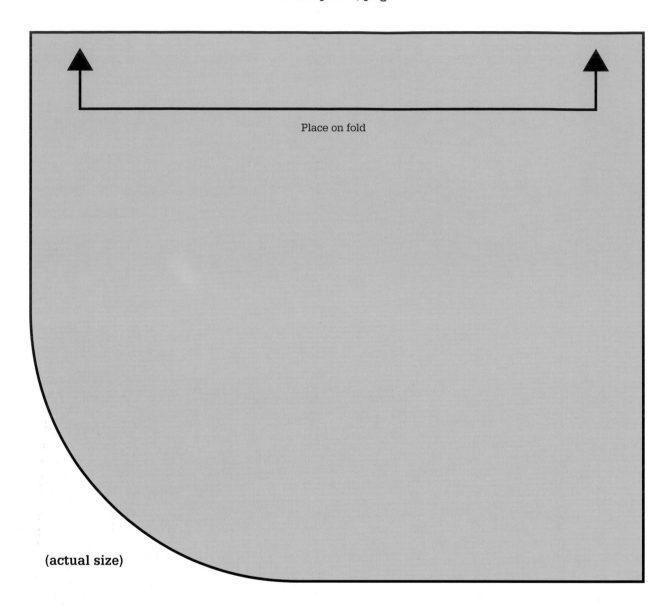

Place on fold

(actual size)

Tapered purse, page 44

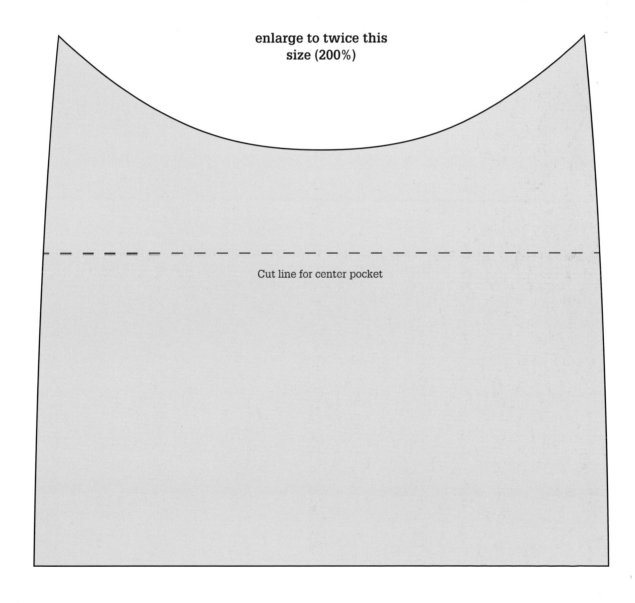

**enlarge to twice this
size (200%)**

Cut line for center pocket

Bucket handled bag, page 16

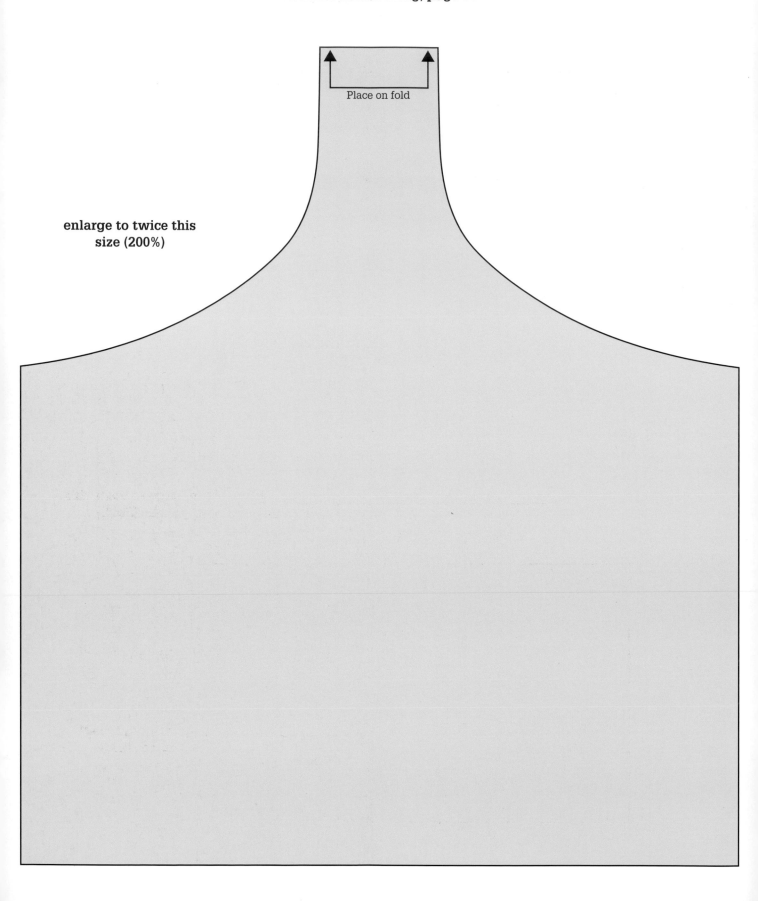

Place on fold

enlarge to twice this
size (200%)

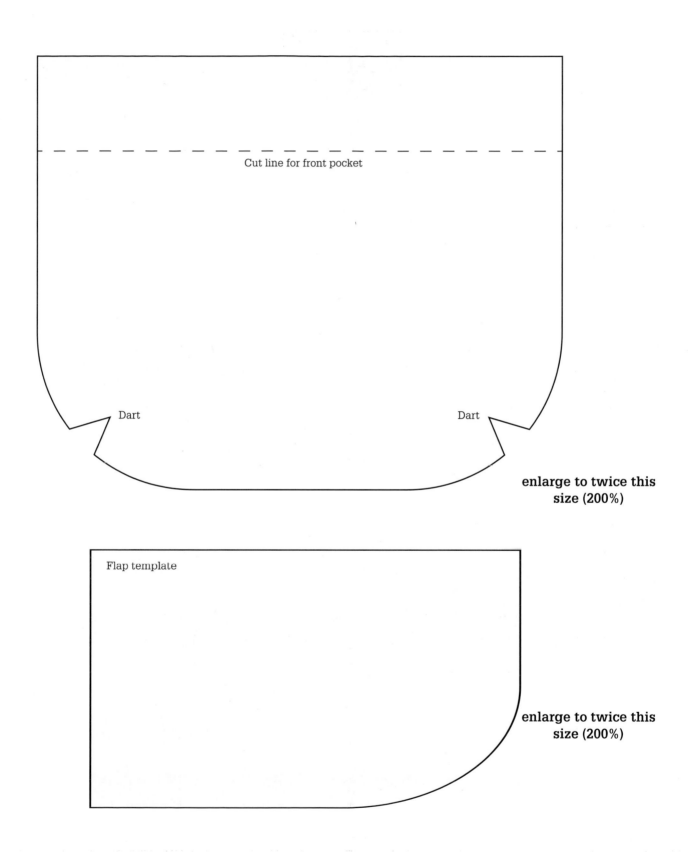

Cut line for front pocket

Dart

Dart

**enlarge to twice this
size (200%)**

Flap template

**enlarge to twice this
size (200%)**

photo transfers

Scan these photo transfer images at 300dpi into your computer and use an image editing program to enlarge them to the size you require, print them out onto photo-transfer paper to be ironed onto your fabric according to the manufacturer's instructions. The images are backward/reversed because they are ironed on face down and will appear the right way around once they are on your fabric.

Simple coin purse—postcard, page 96
this image needs to be printed out at 4 x 6in (10cm x 15cm)

Mini tote bag—bunting, page 102
each piece of bunting needs to be printed out at 2 x 2¼in (5 x 5.5cm)

suppliers

United Kingdom

Abakhan Fabrics, Hobby & Home
111-115 Oldham Street
Manchester
M4 1LN
+44 (0) 161 839 3229
enquiries@abakhan.co.uk
www.abakhan.co.uk
Fabric and bag hardware store

Art2ScreenPrint
Greenway, Hollywood Lane
West Kingsdown
Kent
TN15 6JG
+44 (0) 1474 850559
sales@art2screen.co.uk
www.art2screen.co.uk
Screen printing equipment

The Cloth House
47 Berwick Street,
London
W1F 8SJ
+44 (0) 20 7437 5155
www.clothhouse.com
Fabrics, vintage buttons, and braids

Ebay.co.uk
You can find all the equipment to
handprint and make your own bags here

Fred Aldous Ltd
37 Lever Street
Manchester
M1 1LW
support@fredaldous.zendesk.com
+44 (0) 161 236 4224
www.fredaldous.co.uk
Craft materials and fabric paint

George Weil & Sons
Old Portsmouth Road
Peasmarsh
Guildford
GU3 1LZ
+44 (0) 1483 565800
esales@georgeweil.com
www.georgeweil.com
Rubber carving blocks and craft supplies

Handprinted.co.uk
+44 (0) 1243 697 606
www.handprinted.co.uk
Online printing supplier

JOHN LEWIS
+44 (0) 20 7629 7711
www.johnlewis.com
Department store with branches across
the UK

Rainbow Silks
85 High Street
Great Missenden
Bucks
HP16 0AL
+44 (0)1494 862929
caroline@rainbowsilks.co.uk
www.rainbowsilks.co.uk
Wide range of silk fabrics

T N Lawrence & Son Ltd
208 Portland Road
Hove
BN3 5HR
+44 (0) 1273 260260
www.lawrence.co.uk
Printing suppliers

U-handbag
35 Lower Market St
Hove
East Sussex
BN3 1AT
+44 (0)1273 747112
www.u-handbag.com
Bag-making hardware and frames

North America

ART SHACK
www.artshack.ca
Canadian supplier of arts and crafts
materials and equipment

Dharma Trading Co.
1604 Fourth St.
San Rafael, CA 94901
USA
+1 (800) 542-5227
www.dharmatrading.com
Textile craft supplies

Ebay.com
You can find all the equipment to
handprint and make your own bags here

Joann's
+1 (888) 739-4120
www.joann.com
Wide range of fabrics and haberdashery
with stores across the US

Hobby Lobby
+1 (800) 888-0321
shop.hobbylobby.com
Online arts and crafts store with branches
across the US

Michael's
+1 (800) 642-4235
www.michaels.com
Arts and crafts supplier with stores
across the US and Canada

Rex Art
+1 (800) 739-2782
www.rexart.com
Arts and crafts supplies and materials

Fabric Land
www.fabricland.ca
Large selection of fabrics with stores
across Canada

index

acknowledgements

I would like to say a huge big thank you to everyone who helped make this book happen. All the lovely people at CICO Books—Clare Sayer, Carmel Edmonds, Lindsay Kaubi, Anna Galkina, and Sally Powell. Carrie Hill for the beautiful illustrations and Claire Richardson for photographing my little bags so well.

Thanks to Charlotte and Lucy for their endless support and laughter when much needed, thanks to my family for putting up with me, working all hours, and often covered in paint and loose threads.

Finally thanks to my mum for inspiring me with her creativity, long may we have too many craft projects on the go, mum! x